A NEW APPROACH

THIRD EDITION

Islam

Jan Thompson

Hodder Murray

A MEMBER OF THE HODDER HEADLINE GROUP

For Nicolas McDowall of Edward Arnold, with gratitude for publishing my first book The Christian Faith and its Symbols *(1979), and for encouragement over many years of writing for Religious Education.*

AUTHOR'S NOTES

Arabic words are spelt in English according to the *Glossary of Terms* published by SCAA in 1994, and recommended to publishers to try to standardise spellings.

English Interpretations of the Arabic Qur'an are taken from either *The Koran Interpreted* by A. J. Arberry or *The Meaning of the Glorious Koran* by M. M. Pickthall, unless otherwise stated.

CE stands for Common Era and BCE for Before Common Era.

The Publishers would like to thank the following for permission to reproduce copyright material:
Ahmad Al-Rubaye/Getty Images: p. 95; Circa Photo Library/ William Holtby: p. 29; Circa Photo Library/ © B J Mistry: p. 22 (right); Circa Photo Library/John Smith: pp. 39, 67 (top), 117; Paul Gateshill: p. 6 (right); © Lindsay Hebberd/CORBIS: p. 56; © Chris Hellier/CORBIS: pp. 6 (left), 102; HSBC bank plc: p. 69; © Hanan Isachar/CORBIS: p. 100; © Charles & Josette Lenars/CORBIS: p. 92; © Chris Lisle/CORBIS: p. 26 (left); London Aerial Photo Library/CORBIS: p. 9; © Peter MacDiarmid/ Reuters/CORBIS: p. 110; © Christine Osborne/CORBIS: p. 17 (top); PA photos: p. 83; © Jose Fuste Raga/CORBIS: p. 46; © Reuters/CORBIS: pp. 22 (left), 36, 51; Rex Images: pp. 94, 97, 109; N Roberts/ World Religions Photo Library: p. 96; Ricki Rosen/CORBIS SABA: p. 120; Peter Sanders: pp. 24, 28, 31, 34, 65, 72 (top), 75, 76, 78, 79, 80, 82, 84 (left), 85, 105; © Ted Spiegel/CORBIS: p. 84 (right); © Arthur Thévenart/CORBIS: pp. 3, 4 (left); Jan Thompson: pp. 2, 4 (top right), 5 (left), 7, 26 (right), 30, 41, 50, 62, 68, 77, 115; Rebecca Thompson/ Nomad Images: pp. 1 (left and right), 4 (bottom), 5 (top right), 17 (bottom), 40, 42, 44, 49 (top and bottom), 64; © Graham Tim/CORBIS SYGMA: p. 98; © Sandro Vannini/CORBIS: p. 5 (bottom); Werner Forman Archive Ltd: p. 48; © Adam Woolfitt/CORBIS: p. 91; World Religions Photo Library: pp. 25, 57, 61, 67 (bottom), 72 (bottom), 74, 81, 99, 126.

Cheetah Books, extract from *Eid Mubarak* by Nadia Bakhsh; The Christian Education Movement, extract of an interview from *Religious Education Today*, Spring 1988 and extract in *Religious Education Today* by Nadia Bakhsh; Church Times (www.churchtimes.co.uk), caption from *Church Times*; Kenneth Cragg, extract from *Alive to God: Muslim and Christian Prayer* by Kenneth Cragg, Oxford; The *Independent*, extract from edition 2 May 1988, extract from '300 feared dead as fire sweeps Mecca City', 16 April 1997: and extract from 'Saudis clear debris of Mecca's hellish pilgrimage inferno', 17 April 1997; The Islamic Cultural Centre and London Central Mosque, extracts from a newsletter and a leaflet by Dr Sayyed Darsh; Jamil Morris for the extracts from the website www.zahuri.org and the extract from Poem by Jamil Morris; The New Internationalist, extract from *The New Internationalist*, June 1985; Penguin Classics, extract from *The Koran*, 1974; Simon & Schuster, extracts from *The Koran Interpreted* edited by A J Arberry, 1996; *The Times*, extract from 'Early rising on the home front' by William Greaves, 17 August 1987, © NI Syndication, London (17/8/87); Times Educational Supplement, extract from 'Model for Muslim success', *Times Educational Supplement*, 10 October 2003.

All artwork by Barking Dog Art.

Every effort has been made to trace all copyright holders, but if any have been inadvertently overlooked the Publishers will be pleased to make the necessary arrangements at the first opportunity.

Although every effort has been made to ensure that website addresses are correct at time of going to press, Hodder Murray cannot be held responsible for the content of any website mentioned in this book. It is sometimes possible to find a relocated web page by typing in the address of the home page for a website in the URL window of your browser.

Orders: please contact Bookpoint Ltd, 130 Milton Park, Abingdon, Oxon OX14 4SB. Telephone: (44) 01235 827720. Fax: (44) 01235 400454. Lines are open from 9.00–6.00, Monday to Saturday, with a 24-hour message answering service. Visit our website at www.hoddereducation.co.uk.

© Jan Thompson 2005
First published in 2005 by
Hodder Murray, a member of the Hodder Headline Group
338 Euston Road
London NW1 3BH

Impression number   10 9 8 7 6 5 4 3 2 1
Year   2010 2009 2008 2007 2006 2005

Cover photo courtesy of Roger Wood/CORBIS.
Typeset in Berling 10.5pt by Fakenham Photosetting Limited, Fakenham, Norfolk.
Printed in Dubai.

A catalogue record for this title is available from the British Library.

ISBN-10: 0 340 81491 8
ISBN-13: 978 0340 81451 8

Contents

UNIT ONE

Place of Worship: The Mosque

1

KEY WORDS

Allah: Muslim name for God, meaning 'The God'.
imam: prayer leader (who stands 'in the front' of the other worshippers).
khatib: preacher of the Friday sermon.
khutbah: Friday sermon.
Makkah: the holy city of Islam, in Saudi Arabia.
masjid/mosque: Muslim place of worship.
mihrab: alcove showing the direction of prayer, towards Makkah.
minbar: preaching platform.
mu'adhin/muezzin: person who calls Muslims to prayer.
qiblah: direction for prayer, towards Makkah.

KEY QUESTION

What are mosques and how are they used?

WHAT IS A MOSQUE?

A **mosque** is a Muslim place of worship. It is called a **masjid** in Arabic, the language of Islam. This word literally means 'place of prostration' because, strictly speaking, a mosque is anywhere a Muslim kneels down to prostrate him or herself in prayer. A prayer mat laid down at home, or even at the side of the road, becomes a mosque – a place of prostration.

▲ Muslims prostrate themselves in prayer.

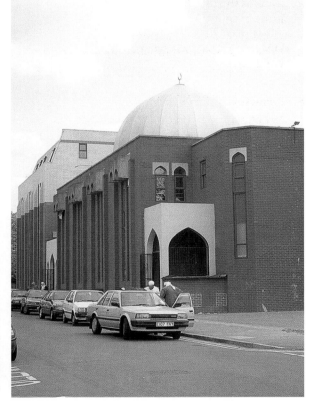

▲ A typical mosque in the UK, in Croydon, Surrey.

We can learn a lot about Islam from mosques. Let's start with the word 'masjid', meaning 'prostration.' When Muslims prostrate themselves in prayer, they show that they have surrendered their lives to God/**Allah**. A Muslim is literally 'one who surrenders' to Allah; and the word islam means 'surrender'. Islam also means 'peace' because it comes from the Arabic 'to make peace' (e.g. by surrendering). Muslims believe that true peace of mind can only come from submission to Allah's will, since they believe he is the Creator and knows what is best for all of his creation.

Once a place is set aside for use as a mosque, then it is subject to a number of rules. Congregational prayers must be held there five times a day, and Muslims must be clean when they enter the mosque. This is because the building is regarded as belonging to Allah.

A mosque has three uses: (1) a place of worship; (2) an Islamic school or college; (3) a community centre, used for all kinds of activities, including a mortuary. Its rooms and facilities must meet all these needs.

WHAT DO MOSQUES LOOK LIKE?

It may be difficult to recognise mosques in non-Muslim countries because, for example, they may be converted houses, redundant church buildings or even fire stations. The only distinguishing feature on the outside may be the notice-board. Mosques which are purpose-built, however, will probably have the traditional external features of a domed roof and minaret. Some elaborate mosques have many domes and minarets. There are also some special features inside mosques. Let's find out what they are for and what they can tell us about Islam.

The dome

This is an important feature of buildings in hot countries because it allows the air to circulate. Islam comes from the Middle East, where the climate is very hot. The dome is built over the prayer hall as it also helps to amplify the human voice.

The minaret

This is a tall tower. In Muslim countries the call to prayer five times a day comes from the top of the minaret. This call rings out over the roofs of other buildings. It is like an alarm clock, reminding people when it is time to pray. Regular daily prayer is obviously very important in Islam. Originally, a man called a **mu'adhin/ muezzin** would climb the tower each time, to give the prayer call. Now recordings and loudspeakers tend to be used.

▲ Mosques can be recognised by their domes and minarets. This is in Jordan.

▲ The star and crescent can be clearly seen atop this minaret.

The star and crescent

Sometimes the dome and minaret of the mosque have a moon-shaped crescent on top of them, or a star and crescent. This five-pointed star and crescent is the main symbol of Islam, depicted on the flags and stamps of many Muslim countries.

- The five-pointed star symbolises the Five Pillars of Islam, i.e. the five basic duties of Muslims.
- The moon and stars are signs to Muslims of the greatness of the Creator.

You will learn that Muhammad (the greatest prophet of Islam) and his early followers were desert people. For them the new moon marked the beginning of each new month, and the waxing and waning moon told them what time of the month it was. A new day did not start at midnight, but in the evening with the appearance of the moon. Islam still uses this lunar calendar.

The positions of the stars were used for guidance by desert people who travelled when it was cool at night and rested in the heat of the day. Stars were also used for finding the direction of **Makkah**, the holy city of Islam. Astronomy became an important Islamic science; with the minaret as an ideal astronomical observatory. By the tenth century Muslims had invented the astrolabe, an instrument with which they calculated the movements of stars and planets. They were able to tell the time of night from this – the forerunner of the modern clock.

TEST YOURSELF

A B C

1. What is the main purpose of a mosque?
2. What does the word 'mosque' or masjid literally mean?
3. Whom do Muslims worship?
4. What are the two external features of a mosque?
5. What are minarets used for?
6. What is the main symbol of Islam?

▲ The prayer hall is a large, carpeted room. This one is in Qabous Mosque in Ibra, Oman.

▲ A screened-off area where women can pray in a mosque in Northern Cyprus, with prayer beads provided.

WHAT ARE MOSQUES LIKE INSIDE?

The prayer hall

There isn't a lot to see in the prayer hall, even though this is the most important part of a mosque. It is simply a large space for the men to gather for prayer. In hot countries this might just be an open courtyard. There are no seats because Muslims need room to go through the prayer movements and prostrate themselves on the floor.

The women's worship area

Women do not have to attend mosques, and often their family responsibilities will prevent them from doing so. If they do attend, they will worship and prepare for worship separately from the men, so that men and women do not distract each other. Often there is a balcony at the back of the prayer hall for the women. Their worship area will be smaller than the men's, since fewer women attend mosques.

▲ A Muslim boy removes his shoes before going to prayer.

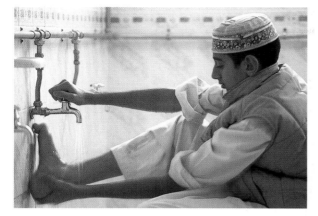

▲ Washrooms are provided at mosques.

Washing facilities

People do not want to prostrate themselves on a dirty floor, so it is important to keep the prayer hall clean. This is also done out of respect for Allah. Washing one's feet also shows respect for the other worshippers. Outdoor shoes are removed before entering and left in the shoe-racks provided. Visitors do not have to wash before going into a mosque, but Muslims going there to pray have to wash thoroughly before-hand. Facilities must be provided for this. If there are washrooms, there will be separate ones for men and women or, in hot countries, there may be two separate fountains or taps in the courtyard.

Carpeting

Some Muslims will use individual prayer mats, but the prayer hall will be carpeted anyway, so that it is comfortable to walk on in bare feet, and to sit and kneel on. Sometimes mosques have special carpeting that has been designed to look like lots of individual prayer mats.

The prayer mat usually has an arch design on it, so that the mat can be laid down in the correct direction for prayer, pointing towards the Ka'bah in Makkah, the holy city of Islam. This direction is called the **qiblah**. The mat shown has a picture of the Ka'bah placed centrally in the top section. This large, cube-shaped building stands in the centre of the Sacred Mosque in Makkah. The Qur'an states that Muhammad, the supreme prophet of Islam, worshipped here.

▲ This prayer mat has a compass on it to find the direction of the Ka'bah (depicted on the mat).

▲ A mosque in Israel is carpeted with rolls of prayer mats.

▲ A traditional mihrab (alcove) and minbar (preaching platform) in Sokullu Mehmet Pasha Mosque in Istanbul, Turkey.

▲ A simpler mihrab and minbar in a UK mosque in Woking, Surrey.

The mihrab

Muslims will know the qiblah as all mosques have a **mihrab**, which is an alcove in the wall. If Muslims face it when they pray, they will be facing in the direction of the Ka'bah. It also serves the useful purpose of amplifying the voice of the **imam** who leads the prayers, facing in the correct direction, with his back to the rest of the worshippers.

The minbar

The only piece of furniture required in a mosque is the **minbar**. This is a set of at least three steps to raise the person (usually the imam) who preaches the Friday midday sermon, so that he can be seen and heard. In large mosques the minbar may be very high and ornate, with a small platform at the top.

TASK BOX

Discuss the following, giving reasons for your views and thinking about alternative views:

a) Do you think Muslims are right to separate men and women in mosques?
b) Do you think Muslims in non-Muslim countries should feel free to pray in the street?
c) Do you think it is necessary to have somewhere special for the worship of God?

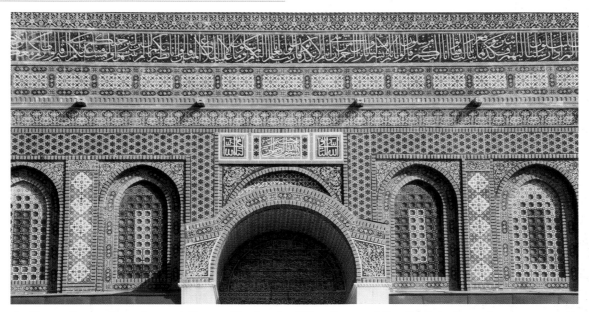

▲ Decorative calligraphy and tiles on the front of The Dome of the Rock in Jerusalem.

Some mosques are beautifully decorated with intricate patterns; others are plain. In either case, there will be no pictures or statues, because of the risk of idolatry – of worshipping images instead of the true God. Islam teaches that Allah is too great to be portrayed by human hands, and therefore forbids any images of him. Figurative art is also discouraged because Muslims are taught that God alone is the creator. Therefore, if they depict any parts of nature, such as a plant, they must make it two-dimensional and highly stylised, rather than try to recreate the real thing. Even when making intricate patterns, there will always be a deliberate mistake, because Muslims believe that only God is perfect.

Decoration on the walls of the mosques often takes the form of passages from the Islamic holy book, the Qur'an, in beautiful writing (calligraphy), which Muslims believe to be Allah's words. Beautiful repeated patterns also represent for some Muslims the idea that Allah has no beginning and no end. They may be geometric designs or the fascinating interweaving of leaves in a floral pattern, known as arabesque. The harmony of these intricate designs represents the order and balance in God's creation and of the unity intended for humanity.

What else might you see in a mosque?

- Notices pinned up on the walls for people to read, such as posters for Muslim Aid – a charity that helps needy Muslims in poor countries.
- Clock faces, showing the times of prayer (this is explained in the next unit).
- Prayer beads, used by some Muslims for private prayer (also explained in the next unit).
- A money-box for charity (known as zakah – explained in Unit 5).

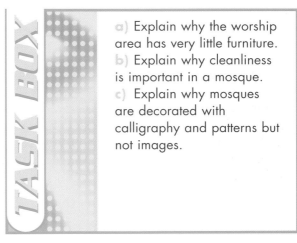

TASK BOX

a) Explain why the worship area has very little furniture.
b) Explain why cleanliness is important in a mosque.
c) Explain why mosques are decorated with calligraphy and patterns but not images.

We have said that a mosque has three basic purposes: a place of worship; an Islamic education centre; and a centre for the Muslim community. Below are some of the 'Regular Activities' advertised for the Islamic Cultural Centre at the London Central Mosque, some of which require special rooms and offices (such as a mortuary, where the dead are brought and prepared for burial).

Regular activities held at the Islamic Cultural Centre, London Central Mosque

Educational

Weekend School
Islamic and Arabic classes for children between the ages of 5 and 15 are held on weekends. Children can either attend on Saturdays or Sundays from 10a.m. to 3p.m. in a school in Acton. For further information contact Sheikh Gamal Manna or Mr Aman. There is a Parent/Teacher Association which is actively involved in assisting the school.

Arabic Classes for Adults
These are held every Sunday from 3 to 5p.m. The classes are taught by Sheikh Ashraf, Sheikh Nassar who should be contacted for further information or any time changes.

Social and Welfare

Counselling
The imams of the Centre are Sheikh Ashraf, Dr Ridwa, Sheikh Nassar and Sheikh Hamdy. They are available at the Centre to discuss any personal problems and difficulties which individual Muslims may have. The imams are normally available from 10a.m. to 3p.m. every weekday except Tuesdays and Fridays.

Marriages
During the month the number of marriages solemnised was twenty.

Visits to Prisons
Delegated imams and persons from the Jamaat (the congregation) visit prison inmates to provide instruction in Islam and perform rehabilitation work. The Centre provides free Islamic literature to them.

Hospital Visits
The Centre would welcome volunteers to visit patients in hospital. Interested persons are asked to contact the Director.

Other Facilities

The Library
The library of the Centre on the upper floor has a wide selection of books and magazines in English, Arabic and other languages. It is only used as a reference library. It is open during normal office hours excepting Saturdays.

Bookshop
The Bookshop has a wide selection of books in Arabic and English on Islam. Audio cassette recordings of the Qur'an are also available.

Funeral Services
The Centre now outsources funeral services ... Expenses are kept to a minimum and must be borne by the estate or relatives of the deceased.

Orientation for Police
Every fortnight new recruits from the Paddington Green Police Station come to listen to a talk from one of the Centre's staff members on Islam.

The British Muslim Association
Meets regularly every Sunday at 3p.m.

(ICC Newsletter, No. 36 (updated))

▲ An aerial photo of the London Central Mosque, in Regent's Park.

TASK BOX

a) Make a brief list of the educational facilities at this large mosque.

b) List other activities that require rooms at the mosque, starting with the mortuary where bodies are washed and prepared for burial.

The best way to study mosques is to visit them and talk to the people there. Big centres, like the London Central Mosque, are accustomed to schools visiting them, and issue the following guidelines. You will learn a lot from local mosques, too.

VISITS TO THE MOSQUE AND ISLAMIC CULTURAL CENTRE
- All visits are accompanied by a guide.
- Visitors are reminded that the Mosque is a place of worship and they are asked to behave accordingly.
- As you may be aware it is customary for Muslim women and girls to wear a head cover in the Mosque. It would be appreciated if the appropriate members of your group could wear a scarf or similar head-covering during the visit.
- We would appreciate it if ladies would wear long-sleeved garments of a suitable length (or loose-fitting trousers).
- Before entering the Prayer Hall you will be asked to remove your shoes.
- Smoking is prohibited in the Mosque and surrounding areas.
- No alcoholic drinks are allowed on the premises.
- A complete tour of the Mosque usually takes about 20 minutes and a further 20 or 30 minutes may be devoted to a talk about Islam followed by discussion. The question-time may be prolonged occasionally depending upon the number of questions from the visitors.
- There is no fee attached to the visits.
- We are not able to provide resource packs or worksheets. Some schools prepare their own questionnaires prior to their visits. This proves to be very useful during the discussion that follows the tour of the Mosque. Some free leaflets and booklets on Islam are available on request.
- We find it most convenient to accommodate visits between 10a.m.–4p.m., Monday–Thursday.

TASK BOX

a) Read these guidelines and think of two questions to ask your teacher about them.

b) Write a notice, suitable for display at the entrance to a mosque, telling people what they must do before entering and what rules they should observe there.

The imam

The Arabic word imam means 'in the front'. This describes the main purpose of the imam, who is the man who stands in front of the lines of worshippers, leading them in recital of the set prayers.

An imam has no special training, and he is not ordained as a holy man. There are no priests or monks in Islam, all Muslims being regarded as equal in the sight of Allah. Basically, an imam is an educated man who is chosen by the congregation because he is regarded as a good Muslim and because of his knowledge of Islam and ability to recite the Qur'an properly. Some imams are specially trained at Islamic colleges called Dar al-Ulooms, where students follow a seven-year course in Arabic and Islamic studies.

Apart from leading the prayers, imams often take on other tasks, as the religious leaders of the local Muslim communities. They often act as the **khatib**, the person who preaches the Friday sermon (the **khutbah**). They will teach about Islam to people of all ages, but particularly to the children who need to learn to read the Qur'an in Arabic. They sometimes perform religious ceremonies, and will give people religious advice. You will see from the 'Regular activities at the London Central Mosque' (p.8) that they are also involved in prison visits. In small mosques the imam may well take on these religious responsibilities as well as another job; in big mosques imams are usually employed full-time.

The Life of an Imam

The following interview with Imam Abdul Jalid Sajid, the imam and Director of the Brighton Islamic Centre and Mosque, gives an insight into his work.

Imam, could you tell us about your upbringing?

I was born and grew up in rural Pakistan . . .. My family wanted me to enter government administration so I went to a school where both the religious and secular traditions were taught. I then studied Arabic, including Islam Studies, at Punjab University. From there I went to Dacca University to study both Journalism and Political Science. I became a journalist and also taught Political Studies at a Christian College. In 1974 I was appointed as a full-time lecturer in Political Studies at Punjab University. It was from there that I came to Britain to do a doctorate.

From this background how did you become an imam?

I had no intention of becoming an imam. Having the qualifications, I was often asked to give sermons at the Friday prayers wherever I happened to be. When I came to Britain in 1976 to the LSE [London School of Economics], I joined the Islamic Society and discovered that there was no one qualified to give the khutbah (the formal Arabic sermon). So I gave it every Friday. While doing my studies I also edited a Muslim newsletter and taught children, again because there was no one else. In 1977, at the request of the Brighton Student Group, I started travelling to Brighton every Friday to lead the prayer and give the sermon. All of this was on a voluntary basis. Then, in 1980, two years after my wife had joined me, I was appointed as the full-time imam and Director here and gave up the idea of a lectureship. There was a great need in Brighton and I felt that God was calling me to do this work.

Apart from leading the Friday prayers, what do you do as an imam?

A tremendous amount! Amongst other things, I organise many activities: educational and religious programmes at the mosque, financial and building projects, an Islamic school for children each evening and mid-week classes for other groups. I visit many schools in the area, and speak to many non-Muslim groups. I am also the authorised Muslim prison and hospital chaplain for Sussex.

What is your aim as an imam in a non-Muslim society?

Muslims are a part of British society, which has to realise that it is a multi-faith and multi-cultural society. We must play a full part in this society, always displaying sensitivity, mutual respect and tolerance. Therefore, apart from helping my own community become better Muslims, I see my role as making Islam understood better among non-Muslims, and helping Muslims understand better other religions and ideas. I have spoken in churches and synagogues in the area and this has been reciprocated.

RE Today

TASK BOX

a) Write a job advertisement for a full-time imam at a local mosque, describing what he will be expected to do.

b) Imagine you know someone who has applied for this job, whom you consider to be an ideal person for it. Write a reference for him, explaining in what ways he is suitable.

c) Assuming your friend is appointed, how important do you think his work will be in the community?

d) Using what you have learnt from this interview, write out at least five questions that would be useful if you were to interview another imam.

1 a) Describe the main features of a mosque.

b) Explain how each feature is used in Muslim worship.

c) To what extent is it necessary for Muslims to have special buildings in which to worship?
Give reasons to support your answer, and show that you have considered different points of view.

Assignment

REMEMBER

▶ Masjid (Arabic)/mosque (English) means 'place of prostration', which Muslims do when they pray.

▶ Mosques are used for:
1) worship of Allah,
2) Islamic education, and
3) community activities.

▶ Inside the worship area is a mihrab (to show the direction of prayer) and a minbar (for preaching).

▶ There are no images in mosques because idolatry is the worst sin in Islam.

🕸 www.theresite.org.uk
(for places of worship)

🕸 www.iccuk.org
(for the Islamic Cultural Centre website)

WEBLINKS

2

KEY WORDS

adhan: first call to prayer.

Allahu Akbar: 'God is most great' – frequently used by Muslims.

du'a: personal prayer.

'iqamah: second call to prayer.

Jumu'ah: Friday prayer.

Ka'bah: the building in the centre of the Great Mosque in Makkah, which has the Black Stone embedded in its wall.

khutbah: Friday sermon.

mu'adhin/muezzin: the person who calls Muslims to prayer.

niyyah: intention to pray.

qiblah: direction for prayer.

Qur'an: Muslim holy book.

rak'ah: a prayer cycle.

salah: daily prayer.

salam: peace.

subhah: prayer beads.

wudu: the washing that Muslims perform before prayer.

KEY QUESTION

How and why do Muslims pray?

WHY DO MUSLIMS PRAY?

There are five things which are obligatory (fard) for a Muslim, known as the Five Pillars of Islam. The first of these is to declare their belief in Allah and in Muhammad his Prophet. Next is **salah**, ritual prayer, to be performed five times a day. In this way, Muslims regularly declare their faith in Allah and offer him praise. This is laid down in their holy book, the Qur'an.

Verily, I am God; there is no god but I; therefore serve Me, and perform the prayer of My remembrance.

Qur'an 20:14 (Arberry)

The Perspectives article on the following page may make prayer sound like a terrible burden; but some Muslims liken the prayer times to tea-breaks. We look forward to the breaks in our daily routine and the chance for refreshment and relaxation. In the same way, prayer times clear the mind of immediate concerns like a maths problem, an English assessment or the demands of a job. By washing for prayer, Muslims are refreshed; through the physical actions of prayer, they are relaxed. Most important of all, they can bring their minds back to focus on Allah who is, for them, the reason and purpose of their existence.

TASK BOX

Explain in your own words what the following quotation from the Qur'an says about the purpose of prayer. Why should it have this effect?

'Prayer restrains from shameful and unjust deeds. ... And Allah knows what you do.'

Qur'an 29:45 (The Essential Teachings of Islam, p. 90)

The following article gives us a feel of what it is like in a Muslim home for the first prayer session of the day. Prayer must be important for them to go to so much trouble. Notice that the last paragraph says that prayer 'Is the centrepiece of their faith'. What do you think this means?

The alarm clock rang at 4.30 a.m. and, as usual, it was Purveen who answered its summons. In the bathroom of the family's three-bedroom, terraced house in Southall, Middlesex, she embarked on the ritual of wudu, cleaning teeth, nose, mouth, ears, hands and forearms and, lastly, her feet. Ready now to perform the Fajr prayer, she returned to the bedroom, faced towards the shrine of Kaaba in Mecca, made her Niyyah – the announcement of her intention to pray – read a paragraph from the Qur'an and prostrated herself to Allah.

With a great deal of door banging, shouting and cajoling, Purveen succeeded in raising daughters, Amberin and Zarrin, sons Saad and Yousef and, last of all, her husband from the depths of their slumbers. As an architect with Ealing Borough Council, Ghayas Syed was not due at work until after nine o'clock and, left to themselves, his family would not be disposed to such spectacular early rising. Indeed, within an hour of the alarm ringing, all of them were back in bed and sound asleep.

Like all devout Muslims, however, the Syeds adhere rigidly to the timetable of prayers which is the centrepiece of their faith. There would be four more prayer sessions to be slotted into the Syed family schedule during the day.

William Greaves in The Times

WHEN DO MUSLIMS PRAY?

The five daily prayers are not laid down in any one passage of the Qur'an, although they can be reached by putting the following two passages together. It was left to Muhammad to give more precise details as to their times, and these are found in the *Hadith*, which record what Muhammad said and did.

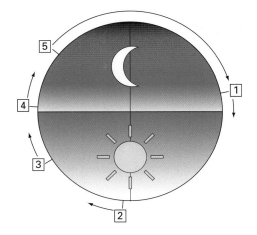

So glory be to God
both in your evening hour
and in your morning hour.
His is the praise
in the heavens and earth,
alike at the setting sun
and in your noontide hour.

Qur'an 30:17–18 (Arberry)

Proclaim thy Lord's praise
before the rising of the sun, and before its
setting, and
proclaim thy Lord's praise
in the watches of the night, and at the ends of
the day.

Qur'an 20:130 (Arberry)

1 **Fajr** – the morning prayer, between dawn and sunrise.
2 **Zuhr** – after midday, during the early afternoon.
3 **Asr** – the late afternoon prayer.
4 **Maghrib** – just after sunset.
5 **Isha** – the night prayer.

Notice that the times are not set *exactly at* sunrise, noon or sunset, to avoid any suggestion of sun worship. However, they are still related to the sun, which changes with the seasons, so they are not always at the same time each day throughout the year. It is important, therefore, for Muslims to know the times of sunrise and sunset each day.

Using the following *Hadith*, explain why it is particularly important for Muslims to pray at the beginning and end of each day:

Ibn Umar reported that the Messenger of Allah (peace and blessings of Allah be upon him) said: 'To offer the prayer in the first hour is to please God and to offer the prayer in late hours is to ask for Allah's pardon.'

Jami' Al-Tirmizi, Selection from Hadith, No. 28, p.17

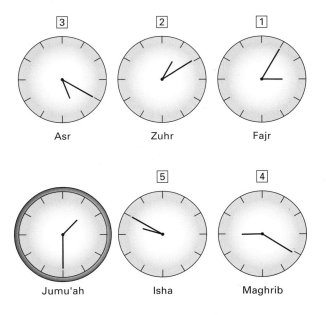

The prayer sessions are quite short, and can take place at any time during the correct periods. If, for any good reason, Muslims are unable to say the prayers at their correct times, then they may say a number of prayers together at the next correct time; however, prayers are not allowed to be said in advance.

> Ibn Mas'ud reported: 'I asked the Messenger of Allah (peace and blessings of Allah be upon him), "Which deed is the most desirable to Allah?" He replied: "To offer the obligatory prayer in time."'

Selection from Hadith, No.27, p.17

Mosques have to decide on the times when they will hold the prayers, for people who are able to come and say them there rather than at home or at work. You might be surprised to see *six* clock faces (on the previous page), showing the times of prayer at a mosque. The sixth one shows the time of the special Friday service, when the **Jumu'ah** prayer takes the place of the Zuhr prayer. *Jumu'ah* is Arabic for 'assembly' or 'congregation'; and Friday, the holy day for Muslims, is called *Yaum ul-Jumu'ah*, the Day of Assembly. All Muslim men should attend mosque on that day, just after noon, to join in the congregational prayer and listen to the sermon (the **khutbah**). Women are not obliged to attend because of their domestic duties.

TEST YOURSELF

1 How many times a day should Muslims pray?
2 What is the Arabic word for this obligatory daily prayer?
3 When is the first prayer session?
4 How many prayer sessions take place after midday?
5 When is the last prayer session?
6 On which day of the week is the Day of Assembly?
7 How many prayer-sessions are there on a Friday?

TASK BOX

a) Explain why the prayer times are not at sunrise, midday and sunset.
b) Can you think of any reasons, particularly for Muslims living in non-Muslim countries, why they might not be able to perform the prayers at the correct times?

HOW DO MUSLIMS PREPARE FOR PRAYER?

Call to prayer

> O ye who believe! When the call is heard for the prayer of the day of congregation, haste unto remembrance of Allah and leave your trading. That is better for you if ye did but know.

Qur'an 62:9 (Pickthall)

Muslims are called to prayer five times a day by the **muezzin**, who stands facing in the direction of the **Ka'bah** in Makkah. In Muslim countries this call goes out from the top of the minarets, and is broadcast on radio and television. In some non-Muslim countries the call may only be given *inside* the mosque, warning those who have gathered there that prayer is about to begin.

The **adhan** is the first call to prayer. It is in Arabic; but here is an English translation:

'Allah is the Greatest.' (Called four times.)
'I bear witness that there is no god but Allah.' (Called twice.)
'I bear witness that Muhammad is the Messenger of Allah.' (Called twice.)
'Come to prayer.' (Called twice.)
'Come to what is good for you.' (Called twice.)
'Prayer is better than sleep.' (Called twice, but only for morning prayer.)
'Allah is the Greatest.' (Called twice.)
'There is no god but Allah.'

▲ A muezzin in Cairo, Egypt calls the faithful to prayer.

The adhan is announced in plenty of time for people to prepare themselves for prayer at the mosque, if they are going to attend. Then a second call is given by the muezzin as he stands in the front row of worshippers inside the prayer hall. This is called the **'iqamah** and it warns people that prayer is about to start. It has the same words as the adhan, with the addition of 'Prayer is about to begin'. This is said twice after 'Come to what is good for you'. All other lines are said only once this time, apart from 'Allah is the Greatest', which is repeated.

Dressing for prayer

Muslims must be properly dressed for prayer. This means removing their shoes, and being cleanly and decently dressed. Women will therefore cover their bodies and wear a scarf over their heads, leaving only their faces and hands uncovered. Men must be covered from at least the waist to the knees. They do not have to wear anything on their heads, but it is customary to wear a prayer cap, which holds the hair in place during prostrations. The traditional prayer cap is a round cloth cap, often crocheted; the important thing is that it does not have a peak, since this would prevent Muslims bowing down to the ground.

▲ A Muslim boy wearing his prayer cap.

TASK BOX

Discuss the following:

a) Do you agree that prayer is 'good for you'? Consider the reasons given for Muslim prayer. Consider the possible spiritual, moral, social, cultural and physical effects of regular daily prayer.
b) What are the advantages and disadvantages for Muslims in attending congregational prayer, rather than praying on their own?

Ritual washing before prayer

Muslims must wash in a particular way before prayer to make themselves ritually clean. They wash the exposed parts of their body. This washing is called **wudu** and the procedure is shown in the diagrams that follow. Before washing, a Muslim will say 'In the name of Allah, the Compassionate, the Merciful'.

▲ 4 All parts of the face are then washed three times, using both hands.

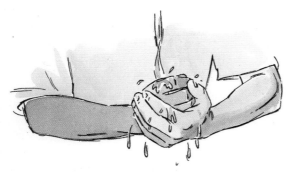

▲ 1 First the hands are washed thoroughly.

▲ 5 The arms, the right first then the left, are washed from wrist to elbow, three times.

▲ 2 The mouth is rinsed out three times.

▲ 6 Wet hands are run backwards over the head, turned over to wipe the neck, and brought round to wipe the ears, inside and out.

▲ 3 Water is snuffed into the nose and blown out, three times.

▲ 7 The feet, the right first then the left, are washed thoroughly up to the ankle.

x

When finished, Muslims make the declaration of faith, 'I bear witness that there is no god but Allah, and Muhammad is the Messenger of Allah'.

If there is no water available for wudu, dry cleaning of the hands, face and arms is an alternative. This is done by touching dust or sand with both hands and then wiping the face and the arms up to the elbows (once).

It is not necessary for Muslims to repeat wudu between prayers if they remain in a state of ritual cleanliness. However, if the person does anything to make them impure, such as passing wind, going to the toilet, or falling asleep, then the wudu must be repeated. A full bath is sometimes necessary before prayer, such as after a wet dream or sexual intercourse.

TEST YOURSELF

1 Who calls Muslims to prayer?
2 How many calls to prayer are there?
3 How should Muslims dress for prayer?
4 What is wudu?
5 Which parts of the body are normally washed before prayer?

HOW DO MUSLIMS PRAY?

Salah consists of set words which are recited from memory, led by the imam. These are mostly expressions of praise for Allah and quotations from the Qur'an. These words are accompanied by set actions. This cycle of ritual prayers and postures is called a **rak'ah**. Each of the five salah requires a particular number of these units, as follows:

Fajr – 2
Zuhr – 4
Asr – 4
Maghrib – 3
Isha – 4

It is best to see salah for yourself (perhaps on video), for the full impact of the flow of the Arabic words and movements. But the diagrams on pages 20–21 will help you to think about the significance of each position.

Prayer direction

Muslims face in the direction of the Ka'bah when they pray. If they are in a strange place, this direction, the **qiblah**, can be found by using a special Islamic compass. If they are at a mosque, they will line up, shoulder to shoulder (men with men and women with women), facing the mihrab, and behind the imam. This shows their solidarity with each other.

> We have seen the turning of thy face to heaven (for guidance, O Muhammad). And now verily we shall make thee turn (in prayer) toward a qiblah which is dear to thee. So turn thy face toward the Inviolable Place of Worship, and ye (O Muslims), wheresoever ye may be, turn your faces (when ye pray) toward it.
>
> *Qur'an 2:144 (Pickthall)*

Prayer intention

The Muslim begins prayer by saying to him or herself that he or she intends to offer this salah. This intention, called **niyyah**, is a conscious effort to focus the mind on Allah and to do the prayer for him. Everything is said in Arabic, but English translations (from *Third Primer of Islam*, pp.14–22) are given on pages 20–21.

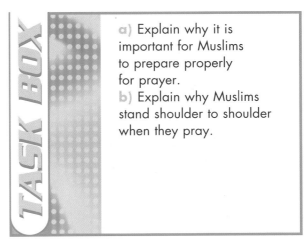

TASK BOX

a) Explain why it is important for Muslims to prepare properly for prayer.
b) Explain why Muslims stand shoulder to shoulder when they pray.

Prayer positions

▲ 1 She raises her hands briefly to her ears, with the words '**Allahu Akbar'** ('Allah is the Greatest'). There is the idea in this gesture of putting behind her all other concerns – only Allah remains before her.

▲ 2 In this next position, she says: 'O Allah, Glorified, praiseworthy and blessed is Thy name and exalted Thy Majesty and there is no deity worthy of worship except Thee. I seek refuge in Allah from the rejected Satan.' The opening chapter of the Qur'an is then recited (sometimes silently), followed by another passage from the Qur'an during the first two rak'ahs.

▲ 3 Bowing, as a sign of respect, she says 'Allahu Akbar' and then, three times, 'Glory to my Lord the great'.

▲ 4 While standing upright, which is also a sign of respect, she says:
'Allah has heard all who praise Him.
Our Lord:
Praise be to Thee.'

▲ 5 With the words 'Allahu Akbar', she prostrates herself on the ground and says three times 'Glory to my Lord, the most high'. After sitting back on her heels for a moment, she repeats this. This position is called **sajdah**, and shows the Muslim's complete submission before Allah. This is very significant because the word 'Islam' means both 'submission' and 'peace'. This shows the Muslim belief that inner peace and outward harmony can only come from all God's creatures submitting to his laws. The first rak'ah is now complete. It takes only about a minute to do.

Note the three basic positions: standing (**qiyam**), bowing (**ruku**), and prostrating (**sajdah**). Each of these goes further than the one before it in showing submission to Allah.

▲ 6 After the second rak'ah, she sits back with the left foot bent towards the right one, as shown, and her hands on her knees. In this position, she silently recites further prayers, particularly asking Allah's blessing on Muhammad and Ibrahim.

▲ 7 When the correct number of rak'ahs are completed, she turns her head to the right and then to the left, blessing her fellow Muslims each time with the words, 'Peace be on you and Allah's blessings'. This is called **salam**, which means 'peace'.

Personal prayer

▲ Muslims hold up cupped hands in private prayer, to show that they are asking Allah for things, such as his blessing.

▲ Muslims using prayer beads.

This unit has concentrated on salah, the obligatory prayers, with set words and set forms, which are recited five times a day. There is also **du'a**, personal prayer. This Arabic word literally means 'asking' and, like any believer, Muslims will have special concerns to bring to Allah in prayer, over and above the prayers laid down for them.

Du'a can take various forms. The worshipper can stay seated after salah and say his own prayers in his own language, or recite some Arabic prayers. Or he can do additional rak'ahs. Du'a can be the prayers said by individual Muslims, in their own words, at any time of day. It can be the recitation of the Qur'an while going about one's work. It can be the repetition of prayers on prayer beads.

Muslim prayer beads (called a **subhah**) are threaded quite loosely on a string, and the ends are knotted together, often finishing in a tassle. The telling of prayer beads is done by passing each bead through the thumb and forefinger, to keep count of the prayers.

Each string has 33 or 99 beads (the latter is divided into sets of 33 by three 'rogue' beads). These are used to recite the Ninety-Nine Beautiful Names. These are 99 different attributes of Allah which occur in the Qur'an, such as 'the Compassionate' and 'the Merciful'.

Not all Muslims use prayer beads, but they are particularly important in **Sufism**, which is the mystical movement in Islam. Sufis use the beads to repeat a sacred formula hundreds or thousands of times. Sufism has had a strong influence on Islam generally, and many Muslims use strings of beads to repeat phrases about Allah. On the first 33 beads they repeat 'Subhan Allah', the Arabic for 'Glory be to Allah'; on the next 33 they say 'al-hamdu-li-Llah', which means 'All praise be to Allah'; and lastly, they say 'Allahu Akbar', 'Allah is the Greatest', 33 times, and once more on the end piece.

TEST YOURSELF

1 How many rak'ahs do most prayer sessions have?

2 In which direction do Muslims pray?

3 What are the three basic prayer positions?

4 What do some Muslims use to help them with their personal prayer?

REMEMBER

▶ Salah is ritual prayer, five times a day.

▶ Salah is the Second Pillar of Islam – an important duty for Muslims.

▶ Muslims wash before prayer.

▶ The cycle of prayer movements and words is called a rak'ah. Each prayer session has between two and four rak'ahs.

▶ The most important prayer position is prostration, which shows that Muslims submit their whole lives to Allah.

WEBLINKS

🕷 www.islamicfinder.org
(for prayer times anywhere in the world)

Assignment

1 Describe how Muslims prepare themselves for prayer.

2 Explain the significance of the prayer movements.

3 If someone believes in prayer, do you think they should pray on a regular basis or just when they feel the need?
Give reasons to support your answer, making reference to Islam and showing that you have considered different points of view.

3

Hijrah: the emigration to Madinah.
Jebreel: the Arabic name for the archangel Gabriel.
jihad: holy war.
Khadijah: Muhammad's first wife.
Laylat-ul-Qadr: the Night of Power – when Muhammad first received his revelations.
Madinah: where Muhammad first established an Islamic state.
Makkah: the holy city of Islam.
Maulid ul Nabi: the Prophet's Birthday.
monotheism: belief in one God.
Muhammad: the Messenger of Allah.
Muharram: the first month of the Muslim year.
polytheism: belief in many gods.

KEY QUESTION

Who was Muhammad and why is he so important in Islam?

WAS MUHAMMAD THE FOUNDER OF ISLAM?

By now you will have realised that **Muhammad** is a key figure in Islam. The First Pillar of Islam is the declaration of faith:

> There is no god but Allah, and Muhammad is the Messenger of Allah.

▲ This is the national flag of Saudi Arabia. It has the declaration of Islamic faith written on it. Try to say it in Arabic: *La ilaha illallahu Muhammad-ur-Rasulallah.*

Islam teaches that there were other prophets before him, but that Muhammad had the last word: that he brought the final, perfect revelation from God to humankind.

When Muslims utter his name, they usually bless him with the words, 'Peace be upon him' (PBUH). So he was aptly named 'Muhammad', since it means 'the Blessed One' or 'the Praised One'. Muslims look back on Muhammad as the ideal man, and they try to live up to his example of faith and goodness.

For all his importance, Muhammad is not seen as the founder of Islam. There are a number of reasons for this:

- Muslims regard their religion as the natural way of life: the way Allah made people and intended them to live. Therefore, Allah himself is seen as the originator of this religion; and Adam, as the first person on earth, is seen as the first Muslim.
- The prophets of Islam go right back to Adam. The great prophet Ibrahim (Abraham) for example, who lived about 2500 years before Muhammad, is called a 'Muslim' in the Qur'an (3:60). Remember that a 'Muslim' is someone who 'submits' to the One God; and Jewish, Christian and Islamic traditions all tell of him rejecting **polytheism** in order to worship the One God. Jews claim to have come from Ibrahim through his son Isaac, and Arabs claim to have come from him through his son Isma'il.

How do Muslims celebrate Maulid ul Nabi – the prophet's birthday?

The Prophet's Birthday is commemorated on 12 Rabi ul Awwal, and the whole of this third month of the Islamic calendar is special because of it. He is said to have died on the same date, 63 years later.

Maulid ul Nabi is sometimes celebrated with a procession through the streets and a communal meal at the mosque. It is a chance for Muslims to listen to a sermon about Muhammad, to retell stories about him to their children, and to ask Allah 'to kindle in us even a spark of that which motivated and impelled him' (in the words of a Friday sermon, close to Maulid ul Nabi).

Despite Muhammad's importance, Muslims are discouraged from making too much of these celebrations, for the following reasons:

- Maulid ul Nabi was not celebrated for the first four centuries of Islam.
- It is feared that rightful respect for Muhammad could turn into worship of him, which would be idolatry. He was, after all, only human; Islam teaches that Allah alone is to be worshipped. For this reason Muslims have never called Islam 'Muhammadanism'.
- Muslims remember Muhammad *every* day: when they hear the call to prayer; when they ask Allah's blessing upon him during salah; and in trying to follow the Prophet's example in every aspect of their lives.

TASK BOX

a) How are Muslims reminded of the Prophet Muhammad in their call to prayer (see p.16)? Quote the relevant lines.
b) Explain why Muslims show Muhammad so much respect.
c) Explain why it would be wrong to call Muslims 'Muhammadans'.
d) In what sense is Adam regarded as a Muslim?
e) Why does the Qur'an call Ibrahim a Muslim?

▲ Muslims celebrate Maulid ul Nabi (photo taken in the U.A.E.).

WHAT WAS MUHAMMAD'S BACKGROUND?

Muhammad was born in **Makkah** in Arabia, over 1400 years ago (about 570CE). Makkah was the centre of the economic and religious life of western Arabia, situated as it was on the junction of the main trade routes between Yemen in the southern tip of Arabia, and Syria and Iraq to the north of Arabia. Muhammad was born into the Hashimite family, which was part of the powerful Quraish tribe, whose headquarters were in Makkah.

Like many Arabs from Makkah, his father Abdullah made his living by trading; it was on his travels that he was taken ill and died in the city of Yathrib only a few months before Muhammad was born. Muhammad, too, was to work as a trader, leading camel caravans across the deserts. And, like his father, he was also to die and be buried in Yathrib (which became **Madinah**).

Tradition tells that the baby Muhammad was sent to a wet nurse in the desert, according to custom, to benefit from the pure desert air. On

returning to the crowded city of Makkah, he had only a few years with his mother, Amina, because she died when Muhammad was six years old. His grandfather, Abdul Muttalib, then took charge of him. He was an important leader in Makkah, and is said to have taken the young boy with him to meetings held in the shade of the Ka'bah.

The old man had only a few more years to live, leaving Muhammad in the care of his son, Muhammad's uncle, Abu Talib. He was to give the orphan love and protection, even in later years when Muhammad made many enemies in Makkah. As he grew up, Muhammad sometimes looked after his uncle's sheep. Sometimes he went with his uncle on trading expeditions.

▲ Arab shepherds with their sheep.

A number of stories surround Muhammad in this period of his life. One tells how he and his uncle stopped at a Christian monastery on their travels, and a monk named Bahira recognised the mark of a prophet on Muhammad's shoulder. Such stories suggest that Allah was preparing Muhammad, in these early years, for his future work.

As a young man, Muhammad showed his concern for justice by becoming a founder-member of a league to protect the safety and rights of strangers in Makkah. He also earned the reputation of being an honest and reliable businessman, and was called **al-Amin**, 'the Trustworthy'. He was too poor to own his own camel caravan, but he so impressed **Khadijah**, the rich widow for whom he worked, that she proposed to him. Despite the age gap (she was 40 years old, and Muhammad 25), they had a very happy marriage. Although polygamy was practised, Muhammad took no other wife while Khadijah was alive.

What was Arabian religion like in Muhammad's time?

Makkah was not only a thriving trading centre, but also a holy city. Once a year, the Arab tribesmen converged on Makkah for a pilgrimage. They came to worship and sacrifice animals to the many idols there, which represented their gods and goddesses. In Makkah, three goddesses were given particular honour: Al-Lat the sun-goddess; Al-Uzza the goddess of the planet Venus; and Manat the goddess of good luck. Allah was also worshipped. His name means 'The God', suggesting that he was the supreme, Creator God; but it seems that he had been eclipsed for most Arabs at that time by their many tribal gods.

Of particular interest in Makkah was the Ka'bah, a cube-shaped building which housed some of their 365 idols. It had a stone embedded in its wall, which the Arabs considered to be sacred. The Quraish tribe had custody of the sacred Ka'bah.

Muhammad, like some other Arabs at that time who were called **Hanifs**, became a **monotheist**, believing that there was only one God, Allah. He rejected the minor gods and goddesses represented by the idols; nor would he worship the spirits which were believed to

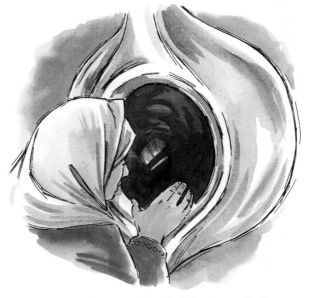

▲ The Black Stone embedded in the wall of the Ka'bah.

haunt natural places like springs, trees, mountains and the winds. (These were called **jinn**, which is where our word 'genie' comes from.) Muhammad could have been influenced in his beliefs by the religions of Judaism and Christianity, which also teach that there is only one God. He would have come across these religions on his travels outside Arabia. There were also some Arab tribes which had converted to Judaism, and there were a few scattered Christian monasteries and holy men in Arabia, seeking the peace and seclusion of the desert.

HOW DID MUHAMMAD BECOME A PROPHET?

▲ Cave Hira on the Mountain of Light.

Muhammad was a thoughtful man and sometimes spent whole nights in prayer. He liked to be alone and would go to the Cave Hira on a mountain five kilometres from Makkah, called Jabal al-Nur, which means 'Mountain of Light'.

One night, when he was 40 years old, he had a religious experience which changed his whole life and the history of the world. He claimed to have seen a vision of a huge figure, which was later identified as **Jebreel** (the archangel Gabriel). The angel commanded him to read or recite (the Arabic word has both meanings). Since he was illiterate, he kept protesting that he could not read, until finally, in great agitation, he realised that he must *recite* what the angel told him.

This was the first of many such experiences which continued to the end of his life. This is how Islam got its holy book, the Qur'an (which means 'Recitation') as Muhammad passed on the words which he believed had come from Allah. The opening of Chapter 96 of the Qur'an records the first words which were given.

> **Power**
> In the Name of God, the Merciful, the Compassionate
> Behold, We sent it down on the Night of Power;
> And what shall teach thee what is the Night of Power?
> The Night of Power is better than a thousand months;
> in it the angels and the Spirit descend,
> by the leave of their Lord, upon every command.
> Peace it is, till the rising of dawn.
>
> *Qur'an 97 (Arberry)*

HOW DO MUSLIMS CELEBRATE THE NIGHT OF POWER?

The Night of Power, called **Laylat-ul-Qadr** in Arabic, is an annual commemoration of that first night when Muhammad began to receive revelations of the Qur'an. This brief chapter of the Qur'an describes that first Night of Power:

> **The Blood-Clot**
> In the Name of God, the Merciful, the Compassionate
> Recite: In the Name of thy Lord who created, created Man of a blood-clot.
> Recite: And thy Lord is the Most Generous, who taught by the Pen,
> taught Man, that he knew not.
>
> *Qur'an 96:1–5 (Arberry)*

This first Night of Power is thought to have occurred during the last ten nights of the month of Ramadan, on an odd number. Most Muslims celebrate it on the night of 27 Ramadan. Many spend the whole night in the mosque, reading the Qur'an and offering prayers. It is said that their prayers will be answered on that night. Some Muslims stay at the mosque for the full ten days, devoting this time to prayer, study of Islam and reading the Qur'an.

▲ A Muslim studies the Qur'an during the last part of Ramadan.

What did Muhammad do next?

That first terrifying experience in Cave Hira left Muhammad wondering if the words he heard were really from Allah, or if he was going mad. On returning home, he confided in his wife, Khadijah, who reassured him. She consulted her cousin, Waraqah, who was a Christian. He told Muhammad that he was a Messenger from God.

Others who knew Muhammad well also believed in him: his cousin, Ali; their adopted slave, Zaid; and Abu Bakr, his best friend. In the first few years he made about 50 converts among friends and family.

Then Muhammad began to preach in public, passing on the words that he claimed to have received from Allah. The short chapters of the Qur'an, towards the end of the holy book, are typical of this early period. They denounce idolaters and call on them to worship the One God. Over the next few years his following grew, but so too did the opposition. In 615CE Muhammad sent some of the Muslims into Christian Ethiopia, to escape persecution. The Year of Mourning, 619, was when his beloved wife died, and also his uncle Abu Talib who, although not a Muslim himself, had given Muhammad the family's protection. This was now withdrawn.

TEST YOURSELF

1 Which city was the centre of Arabian religion?
2 Which monotheistic religions may have influenced Muhammad?
3 What is the name of the cave where Muhammad went to pray?
4 Whom did Muhammad see in a vision?
5 What did the angel tell him to do?
6 What do Muslims call the night when Muhammad had this experience?
7 How do Muslims commemorate it today?

What is Isra'wal Mi'raj?

This commemorates the Night Journey and Ascension, an experience Muhammad had about this time, when he most needed reassurance. It is claimed that in one night he travelled all the way from the Holy Mosque in Makkah to the 'Further Mosque' of Jerusalem. Tradition tells that this miraculous journey was on a winged horse called Buraq, and that Muhammad ascended into heaven from the famous rock in Jerusalem over which the Dome of the Rock now stands. There he spoke to the prophets of old and brought back the command to pray to Allah five times a day.

Isra' wal Mi'raj is remembered each year on 27 Rajab. It is celebrated by reading the Qur'an (particularly Chapter 17, 'The Night Journey') and by saying extra prayers that night.

▲ The Dome of the Rock. A mosque was first built here by Caliph Umar in 638CE. This beautiful building dates from 687CE. It covers the huge rock from which Muhammad is believed to have ascended to heaven. The Dome of the Rock is more a shrine than a mosque, and another mosque was built nearby, soon afterwards, with much more room inside for Muslims to gather for prayer. That one is called the Al-Aksa Mosque, meaning 'The Further Mosque', to commemorate the miraculous Night Journey.

A New Approach – Islam

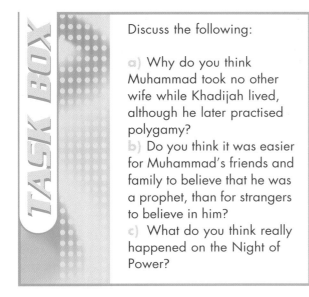

Discuss the following:

a) Why do you think Muhammad took no other wife while Khadijah lived, although he later practised polygamy?

b) Do you think it was easier for Muhammad's friends and family to believe that he was a prophet, than for strangers to believe in him?

c) What do you think really happened on the Night of Power?

WHY DID MUHAMMAD LEAVE MAKKAH?

Matters came to a head in 622CE when there was a serious plot to assassinate Muhammad. By this time his influence had spread 480 kilometres beyond Makkah, to the city of Yathrib. A number of its citizens had been converted to Islam when visiting Makkah on pilgrimage, and they now invited Muhammad to become their leader, hoping he could settle some internal squabbles.

Having put up with hardship and persecution for many years now, Muhammad must have felt that it was the will of Allah for him to leave Makkah. So, on 16 July 622, Muhammad set out by night with Abu Bakr on the journey to Yathrib. This is known as the **Hijrah**, the Arabic word for 'emigration'. Muhammad had already sent on ahead of him over a hundred Muslim families; and more joined them from Ethiopia. The Muslims had the following titles:

- The Companions were all those Muslims who knew Muhammad in his lifetime;
- The Emigrants were all those who had come with him to Yathrib;
- The Helpers were citizens of Yathrib who converted to Islam.

Later, Yathrib was called **al-Madinah**, in Muhammad's honour – 'the Town' (of the Prophet). It was the first Islamic city-state.

▲ The present-day city of Madinah.

Why are Muslim years dated from the Hijrah?

So important was the Hijrah, as the start of the time when a community was first run on Islamic lines, that it became the beginning of the Muslim calendar. Islamic years are dated AH (from the Latin *anno Hegirae* – 'in the year of the Hijrah'). So 622CE became 1AH for the Muslims. Muharram is the first month in the Islamic calendar, so 1st Muharram is New Year's Day. (Muharram 1425 began in February 2004 – see page 56 for an explanation of why Muslim years are shorter than Western years.)

The 1st Muharram commemorates the Hijrah but, like the remembrance of the Prophet's Birthday, it is not seen as an opportunity for wild celebrations, but for remembering the life and example of Muhammad. Muslims attend mosque for special prayers and a sermon about Muhammad's career, especially the event of the Hijrah. Just as Muhammad left behind his enemies in Makkah, so Muslims are encouraged to leave behind them all that is bad in their lives and to try to be better Muslims.

WHAT DID MUHAMMAD ACHIEVE IN MADINAH?

Almost half Muhammad's years of prophethood were spent in Madinah, where he proved himself a very capable leader. He ruled from a simple home which he had helped build and which was adjacent to the first mosque. In Makkah he had preached a basic message of belief in Allah, the One God; that he was Allah's messenger; and that the Day of Judgement was coming. Now, with the establishment of the first Islamic state, the religion became more organised, with detailed instructions about prayer, fasting, charity and pilgrimage. He was also

Months (29/30 days)		Commemorations
1 Muharram	1st	The Day of Hijrah; New Year
2 Safar		
3 Rabi ul Awwal	12th	Maulid ul Nabi (Birthday of the Prophet)
4 Rabi ul Akhir		
5 Jamada al Awwal		
6 Jamada al Akhir		
7 Rajab	27th	Isra' wal Mi'raj (Night Journey and Ascension)
8 Sha'ban		
9 Ramadan	27th	Laylat-ul-Qadr (Night of Power)
10 Shawwal	1st	Id-ul-Fitr (Minor Festival)
11 Dhul Qi'da		
12 Dhul-Hijjah	10th	Id-ul-Adha (Major Festival)

▲ The Islamic calendar.

asked for advice on how to behave in all spheres of life, such as work, leisure and family relations, and he answered either with quotations from the Qur'an or with sayings of his own.

Unfortunately, hostility continued between Makkah and Madinah, and two significant battles were fought. In 624 the Muslims, although outnumbered, won a resounding victory at the Battle of Badr. But in the following year, they lost the Battle of Uhud against a massive army from Makkah. In 627 the Makkans besieged Madinah; but the city survived, due largely to the digging of a trench around it. Finally a truce was agreed, the Hudaybiya peace treaty, which allowed Muslims to visit the holy city of Makkah on pilgrimage. By 630, the treaty having been broken by the Makkans, the Muslims were strong enough to advance on Makkah with a huge army of 20,000 men. There was no resistance. Muhammad generously spared his enemies, but insisted that the idols of Makkah be destroyed. He had reclaimed the holy city for Allah.

HOW MANY WIVES DID MUHAMMAD HAVE?

It is thought that Muhammad took 12 wives in all, during his time at Madinah. Remember that polygamy was perfectly acceptable in Arabia at that time. Many of his new wives were the widows of his followers who had been killed in battle and who now had no one to protect them. Other wives came through marriage alliances as Muhammad extended his influence over more and more Arab tribes.

Ayesha, the daughter of his closest friend, Abu Bakr, was the only one who had not been married before. When Muhammad had been married to Khadijah his first wife, he had taken no others. They had had six or seven children (although only his four daughters had survived into adulthood). Now, in Madinah, with his many wives, only one more child was born to Muhammad.

HOW DID MUHAMMAD DIE?

In March 632, Muhammad went on pilgrimage to Makkah for the last time, and delivered his famous farewell speech to his fellow pilgrims. Why do you think this speech became so important for Muslims?

It began:
> 'O People, lend me an attentive ear, for I know not whether, after this year, I shall ever be amongst you again. Therefore listen to what I am saying to you very carefully and take these words to those who could not be present here today.'

Most of the sermon was about human rights, and Muhammad also enforced the five essential practices of Islam, known as the Five Pillars:
> 'O People, listen to me in earnest, worship Allah, say your five daily prayers (salah), fast during the month of Ramadan, and give your wealth in zakah. Perform Hajj if you can afford to.'

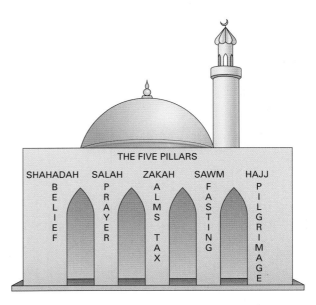

THE FIVE PILLARS

SHAHADAH	SALAH	ZAKAH	SAWM	HAJJ
BELIEF	PRAYER	ALMS TAX	FASTING	PILGRIMAGE

He finished with these words:

'O People, no prophet or apostle will come after me and no new faith will be born. Reason well, therefore, O People, and understand my words which I convey to you. I leave behind me two things, the Qur'an and my example the Sunnah and if you follow these you will never go astray.

'All those who listen to me shall pass on my words to others and those to others again; and may the last ones understand my words better than those who listen to me directly. Be my witness, O Allah, that I have conveyed your message to your people.'

From The Prophet Muhammad's Last Sermon

This became known as the Farewell Pilgrimage because, a few months later, Muhammad died of fever and was buried in Madinah. His tomb is still there, under the green dome of the Prophet's Mosque, with the tombs of his two successors, Abu Bakr and Umar.

TASK BOX

a) Explain why the Islamic dating system uses the letters AH.

b) Why do you think the five main obligatory duties for Muslims are called the Five Pillars?

▲ The Prophet's Mosque at Madinah, illuminated at night.

34

A New Approach – Islam

WHAT IS HOLY WAR?

While they lived in Makkah, the Muslims refused to fight against their enemies, even though they were provoked. But eventually, in Madinah, Muhammad came to believe that war is sometimes right and that to fight in defence of Islam is to fight for Allah.

The first big battle, the Battle of Badr, was fought with just over 300 men and boys against a Makkan force of 1000. The Muslim victory was seen as proof that their religion was right, for Allah was obviously on their side. The Muslims must have felt like David the shepherd-boy who fought for the Lord's people against the giant, Goliath. David is regarded as a prophet in Islam, and his victory is referred to in the Qur'an.

> So they routed them by Allah's leave and David slew Goliath; and Allah gave him the kingdom and wisdom, and taught him of that which He willeth. And if Allah had not repelled some men by others the earth would have been corrupted. But Allah is a Lord of Kindness to (His) creatures.
>
> *Qur'an 2:251 (Pickthall)*

A Muslim commentary on this text says this:

> The essential point is that we must fight for the preservation of our Faith, no matter how overwhelming the odds may seem. In fact, if we fight for Allah with courage and unshakeable belief it is our foes who face overwhelming odds, for Allah has promised He will aid us.
>
> *The Essential Teaching of Islam, p.161*

Islam calls war which is fought for Allah **jihad**, or 'holy war'. The Qur'an teaches that it should only be fought by Muslims in self-defence, or in defence of Islam. It should not be used to try to convert people to Islam, and it should be stopped when the enemy wants peace. Muhammad made further regulations, forbidding civilian casualties. He also set an example of mercy to the conquered. Islam teaches that those who die fighting in holy war will go straight to heaven. This has been a powerful incentive to Muslim soldiers, and an important factor in the success of many Islamic wars. Chapter 2 of the Qur'an makes a number of points about jihad:

> Warfare is ordained for you, though it is hateful unto you; but it may happen that ye hate a thing which is good for you, and it may happen that ye love a thing which is bad for you. Allah knoweth, ye know not.
>
> *Qur'an 2:216*
>
> Fight in the way of Allah against those who fight against you, but begin not hostilities. Lo! Allah loveth not aggressors.
>
> *Qur'an 2:190*
>
> But if they desist, then lo! Allah is Forgiving, Merciful. And fight them until persecution is no more, and religion is for Allah. But if they desist, then let there be no hostility except against wrongdoers.
>
> *Qur'an 2:192–3 (Pickthall)*

Throughout the ages, there have been occasions when some Muslims have felt it right to take up arms for their faith. But for all Muslims there is the greater holy war. The word *jihad* literally means 'striving', and it also describes the effort that Muslims must make to do Allah's will every day of their lives. It means fighting all the evil thoughts and desires within ourselves, like greed, envy, lust and laziness. It means being prepared to do something about the injustices we see all around us, like defending the weak against the bullies, sending money to the starving people in developing countries, speaking out about cruelty to animals or wastage of the world's resources.

Jihad demands sacrifice – sacrifice of one's time, skills, money, even perhaps of one's life. This is the greater Jihad. Jihad is so important that some Muslims regard it as the Sixth Pillar of Islam.

▲ On 11 September 2001 ('9/11') Islamic extremists belonging to an organisation called al-Qaeda mounted attacks on the USA which have since had serious consequences worldwide. This photograph shows the destruction of the twin towers of the World Trade Center in New York. The suicide bombers believed that they were martyrs for their faith, but the Islamic world at large was quick to distance itself from these atrocities in which many innocent people died.

TEST YOURSELF

1 Which battle did the Muslims win against overwhelming odds?
2 Which battle did they lose to the Makkans?
3 What is the Arabic word for holy war?
4 State four conditions for holy war.
5 What is the 'greater holy war'?

TASK BOX

Discuss the following:

a) Do you think war can ever be 'holy'? (Consider: If war is evil, should it ever be used? Does the end ever justify the means?)

b) Why do you think striving against our own faults is regarded as the *greater* holy war?

REMEMBER

- Muslims do not regard Muhammad as the founder of Islam, but as the Messenger of Allah.
- Muhammad had a life-changing experience on the Night of Power.
- Muhammad rejected the idolatry of his time and preached that there was only one God.
- Muhammad established the first Islamic state in Madinah in 622CE.
- Muhammad eventually captured Makkah and made it the centre of Islam.

WEBLINKS

- www.usc.edu/dept/MSA/fundamentals/prophet *(for detailed information on Muhammad)*
- www.themodernreligion.com *(follow the links for Prophet Muhammad's Last Sermon)*

1 Describe Muhammad's call to prophethood.

2 Explain the importance of making Makkah the centre of Islam.

3 How important do you think it is to have a leader to look up to? Give reasons to support your answer and show that you have thought about different points of view. You must take into consideration the role of Muhammad in Islam.

Assignment

4

akhirah: belief in life after death.

Arabic: the language of Islam.

ayah (singular): unit within a surah/chapter of the Qur'an.

Bismillah: 'In the name of Allah ...'. The beginning of a phrase that starts most chapters of the Qur'an. (The first Arabic phrase that Muslim children learn.)

Fatihah: 'The Opening' – first chapter of the Qur'an.

Hadith (pl. ahadith): 'statement(s)' of what Muhammad said and did.

hafiz/hafizah: a man/woman who can recite the Qur'an from memory.

Injil: the Christian Gospel.

khalifah: successor, inheritor, custodian.

qadar: Allah's control over destiny, predestination.

Qur'an: Muslim holy book, believed to contain the actual words of Allah.

rasul: a messenger (of Allah) – often a prophet who brought a holy book.

risala: prophecy.

Shahadah: Muslim profession of faith, the First Pillar of Islam.

shirk: the sin of idolatry, the worst sin.

Sunnah: Muhammad's customary practice, used to guide Muslims.

surah: a chapter of the Qur'an.

tawhid: very important Muslim belief in the oneness of Allah.

Tawrah (or Tawrat): Jewish Torah, the most important Jewish scriptures, attributed to Moses.

Zabur: The Book of Psalms in the Bible, attributed to David.

KEY QUESTION

What scriptures do Muslims use and how important are they?

> I leave behind me two things, the Qur'an and my example the Sunnah and if you follow these you will never go astray.

From The Prophet Muhammad's Last Sermon

WHERE DID THE QUR'AN COME FROM?

Muslims believe that the words of the Qur'an come from Allah himself, and were passed on to humanity through the Prophet Muhammad, so they do not regard Muhammad as its author. Instead, he is believed to have recited accurately the words which were revealed to him by the angel Jebreel (Gabriel), who is also said to have told Muhammad the order in which the passages were to go. People who heard Muhammad jotted down these words on all sorts of scraps of writing material, or committed them to memory. They were collected together into a book immediately after Muhammad's death, under the direction of Abu Bakr, his first successor. Various copies of the Qur'an circulated in its early years until Uthman, the third successor of Muhammad, recalled them and issued standardised copies, based on the original, to the main Islamic cities. All copies since then have been identical.

▲ Illuminated pages of the Qur'an, in Arabic.

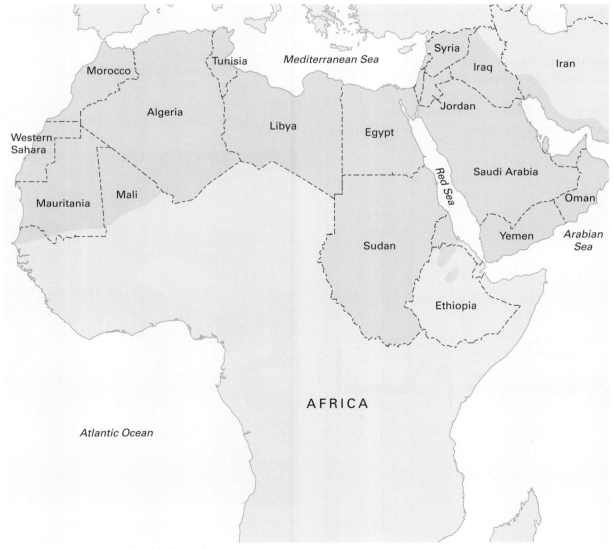

▲ Main areas where Arabic is spoken.

WHY MUST THE QUR'AN BE IN ARABIC?

Since the Qur'an is believed to be from Allah, every word, every letter, is sacred to Muslims. It is therefore considered very important to keep the Qur'an in the language in which it was first spoken, i.e. Arabic. As Islam spread from Arabia, its language was adopted by a number of Islamic countries, and is still spoken in these countries today (as the map shows). Muslims in these countries should find the Qur'an quite easy to read, even though the style of modern Arabic has naturally changed since Muhammad's time.

In other countries, Muslims need to learn enough Arabic to take part in their worship and to read the Qur'an. You can find translations of the Qur'an for people who do not know Arabic, or copies with both Arabic and another language for those who do not have Arabic as their first language; but Muslims do not accept any translation as the proper Qur'an. They regard translations as interpretations rather than the real thing. Translating one language into another must involve an element of interpretation, in trying to choose equivalent words and expressions. For this reason, Islam has insisted that the Qur'an must remain as it was revealed from Allah. It is too precious to risk losing any of its meaning; apart from which, the very sound of the Arabic Qur'an is sacred to Muslims.

Arabic is written from right to left, and books written in Arabic will open in this direction. So the Qur'an looks as if it starts at the back, to those of us who read books in languages which use the Latin alphabet. In the same way, English books look back-to-front to Arabic-speaking people.

As-Salamu-Alaykum, 'Peace be with you'. This ▲ is the common Muslim greeting in Arabic.

What style of writing is it?

The Qur'an is written in verses of different lengths held together by loose rhymes. The beauty and majesty of this language is usually lost in translation, but A. J. Arberry's version, *The Koran Interpreted*, tries to retain the rhythmic patterns of the original.

All but one of the chapters (Chapter 9) begin with the words: 'In the name of Allah, the Merciful, the Compassionate'. This is known as the **Bismillah**, its first word in Arabic: '*Bismillah ir Rahman ir Rahim*'.

Why is it called the Qur'an?

The Arabic word 'Qur'an' means 'recitation', and it is an appropriate title. Muhammad was commanded to recite the words spoken to him by the angel Jebreel. Muslims recite passages of the Qur'an at their five daily prayer sessions. Children are taught how to recite the Qur'an; you can see them nodding their heads up and down to the rhythm of the words. When someone has learnt the whole Qur'an by heart, he is called a **hafiz** and she is called a **hafizah**.

▲ Teenage boys learning the Qur'an at an Islamic school.

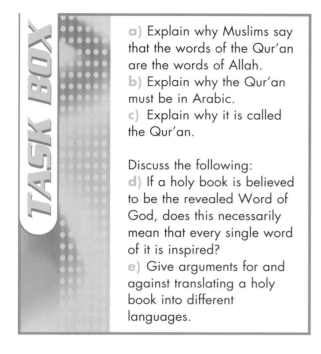

a) Explain why Muslims say that the words of the Qur'an are the words of Allah.

b) Explain why the Qur'an must be in Arabic.

c) Explain why it is called the Qur'an.

Discuss the following:

d) If a holy book is believed to be the revealed Word of God, does this necessarily mean that every single word of it is inspired?

e) Give arguments for and against translating a holy book into different languages.

How is the Qur'an organised?

The Qur'an has 114 chapters, which are called **surahs**. Muslims tend to know them by their titles rather than their numbers. So, for instance, Chapter 1 is 'The Opening' ('Al **Fatihah**' in Arabic); and Chapter 2 is 'The Cow' – named after the story of the yellow cow in verses 67–71. There are over 6000 verses in the Qur'an; but the verse divisions are not always identical, and this can cause problems if you are looking up references. A unit within a surah is called an **ayah.**

 The Opening

In the Name of God, the Merciful, the Compassionate

Praise belongs to God, the Lord of all Being, the All-merciful, the All-compassionate, the Master of the Day of Doom.

Thee only we serve; to Thee alone we pray for succour.

Guide us in the straight path, the path of those whom Thou hast blessed, not of those against whom Thou art wrathful, nor of those who are astray.

The Koran Interpreted (Arberry)

Apart from the opening chapter, the surahs at the beginning of the Qur'an tend to be the longest, with the very short chapters at the end. Chapter 2, for example, is the longest of all the surahs, with 286 verses, many of which are themselves quite long. The last four surahs have only between four and six lines each. Most of the short chapters come from Muhammad's early period in Makkah, when he was preaching a simple message of belief in the One God and warning of God's punishment for idolaters. These surahs are short and sharp. The longer chapters belong to Muhammad's period in Madinah, when the Islamic community needed more detailed guidance.

HOW DO MUSLIMS TREAT THE QUR'AN?

Muslims show their respect for the Qur'an by treating it with great care. They wrap each copy in a clean piece of cloth, or in a special cloth bag which is stitched in the shape of an envelope. They keep it on the highest shelf in the room, to show its superiority, and they would never put anything on top of it. They wash before touching it, at the very least their hands, and some Muslims perform full wudu (see p.18).

▲ Some Muslims use purpose-made wrappers or covers for the Qur'an; others use a piece of clean cloth, as here.

The Qur'an is divided into 30 sections, one for each day, to make it easy to recite it right through during a month. Muslims try to do this especially during the holy month of Ramadan. It is also recited at all special religious celebrations.

TEST YOURSELF

1 What does the word 'Qur'an' mean?
2 In which language is the Qur'an written?
3 Is it in verse or prose?
4 What do you call a boy or man who has learnt the Qur'an by heart?
5 What is the title of the first surah of the Qur'an?
6 What must Muslims do before reading the Qur'an?
7 Name four things that Muslims must not do while reading the Qur'an.

Girls and women cover their heads with a scarf when reading it and boys and men will usually wear a prayer cap. They do this out of respect. As it is customary for Arabs to sit on the floor, a folding bookstand is used when reading the Qur'an, so that the holy book does not touch the ground. Muslims are not allowed to eat or drink, smoke or talk in the same room where it is being read, for they must give it their full attention. If they have any posters or other wall-hangings with words of the Qur'an on them, they are put on a wall which they face, so that they do not turn their backs on them.

How do Muslims read or recite the Qur'an?

The Qur'an is part of a Muslim's daily life. Muslim men and women recite or read it often; some carry pocket-size editions around with them. The opening chapter of the Qur'an is recited at the beginning of each rak'ah (see pp.19–21) at the five daily prayers, and it may be followed by any other passage from the Qur'an.

WHY IS THE QUR'AN SO IMPORTANT?

That is the Book, wherein is no doubt, a guidance to the godfearing.

Qur'an 2:2 (Arberry)

Today I have perfected your religion for you, and I have completed My blessing upon you, and I have approved Islam for your religion.

Qur'an 5:5 (Arberry)

Muslims believe that the Qur'an is a perfect copy of a heavenly book, and that it is the last revelation of Allah's truth to the human world. They believe that it is therefore the best guide we can have in living our lives as Allah intended, and that this is the way to salvation.

A book that trains young Muslim children in their faith sums up the importance of the Qur'an like this:

> It is the Last and Final Book sent by God.
> The Qur'an is a Great Book.
> Its style is beautiful.
> Its language is sweet.
> Its message is full of life.
> It tells us how to worship God.
> It tells us how to live a life of virtue.
>
> A Muslim believes in the Qur'an.
> A Muslim reads the Qur'an.
> A Muslim tries to follow the Qur'an.
>
> *From First Primer of Islam*

WHAT ARE THE HADITH?

Muslims turn first of all to the Qur'an for guidance, but they also have the **Hadith**. The word 'hadith' means a 'statement' or 'report'; and the books of Hadith are collections of reports of what Muhammad said, did or approved in particular situations. Some **ahadith** (plural) are especially important because they record the **sunnah** of Muhammad, i.e. his 'custom', 'practice' or 'way' (of doing things), which he wanted Muslims to follow. So, apart from the rules in the Qur'an, Muslims also have the example of Muhammad himself, showing how the Prophet put the Qur'anic rules and ideals into practice. The precise times of the five daily prayers, for example, are laid down in the Hadith, but are not made clear in the Qur'an. The Qur'an itself says: 'You have had a good example in God's Messenger.' (33:21)

PERSPECTIVES

In the following quotation, a Muslim explains the importance of the Qur'an. Note down the main points that she makes about its relevance for today.

The Qur'an is an old book and the translations into English leave much to be desired. It is not written down in any logical order and there is much apparent repetition. It is like a goldmine with nuggets of wisdom waiting at every turn to be discovered and treasured – and the gold is as bright today as it was fourteen centuries ago.

All that we struggle for today was also the struggle, the jihad, then. Justice, compassion for the weak and oppressed, women's rights, equitable distribution of property, concern for the environment and the sanctity of life.

Even its penal *(legal)* code, much maligned of late as barbaric, makes provision for offenders to be encouraged to ask forgiveness and gives them several opportunities to change their ways before the ultimate penalties are imposed. It bears a resemblance to some of the more humane societies of today which try to re-educate offenders to a sense of their social responsibilities.

The vision of the Qur'an is based upon a clear decision to believe in God. And it invites others to make that decision, promising great spiritual rewards. . . .

Muhammad was under no illusion that everyone would agree with him or accept what he said. Nor did he try to force anyone to agree. But such was the power of his vision that it did eventually succeed in capturing the imaginations of even his worst enemies. It still continues to inspire many young (and old) reformers today as well as influencing the day-to-day lives of Muslims everywhere.

Harfiyah Ball in New Internationalist

▲ A boy reads from the Hadith in a Muslim library.

TEST YOURSELF

1 Name two things Muslims do to show respect for their copies of the Qur'an.
2 Which is the most frequently quoted chapter (surah) of the Qur'an?
3 What is a hadith?
4 Name one of the compilers of the Hadith.
5 What is the main difference between the Qur'an and the Hadith?

KEY QUESTION
What are the main beliefs of Islam?

Notice that there is a firm distinction made between what Muhammad said when he claimed to be passing on revelations that had come to him from Allah, which form the Qur'an, and when he was giving his own teaching which is recorded in the Hadith.

Each Hadith records both the information about Muhammad and its chain of transmission, for example, 'X reported that Y reported that Z reported that Uthman reported that the Messenger of Allah (PBUH) said . . .' The chain is not usually quoted today, only the text: 'Uthman reported that the Messenger of Allah (peace and blessings of Allah be upon him) said: The best amongst you is the person who learnt Al-Qur'an and taught it.' (Bukhari; *Selection from Hadith*, No.102, p.55.)

Most Muslims accept six books of Hadith as being the most trustworthy. These are known as The Accurate Six and were collected within the first three centuries of Islam. The two most authoritative books are called **sahih**, meaning 'sound'; they are Sahih Al-Bukhari and Sahih Muslim.

WHAT ARE THE MUSLIM ARTICLES OF FAITH?

The following verse from the Qur'an sums up the Five Articles of Faith (**iman**) in Islam, which it says have been revealed or 'sent down' from Allah. It speaks of belief in:

- God (Allah)
- His angels
- His books
- His messengers (the Prophets)
- 'The homecoming' (life after death)

The Messenger believes in what was sent down to him from his Lord,
and the believers; each one believes in God and His angels,
and in His Books and His Messengers; we make no division
between any one of His Messengers. They say, 'We hear, and obey.
Our Lord, grant us Thy forgiveness; unto Thee is the homecoming.'

Qur'an 2:285 (Arberry)

Why is belief in the one God so important?

The first Article of Faith is the same as the first Pillar of Faith: belief in Allah, the One God (Allah means 'The God'). The first Pillar can be called both the **Shahadah** and the **Kalimah**. Shahadah comes from the Arabic *ash-hadu*, meaning 'I declare'; and it describes a profession of faith. Kalimah is the term used for a statement of faith. (Strictly speaking, there are two kalimahs in the declaration that: 'There is no god but Allah, and Muhammad is the Messenger of Allah.')

The first Article of Faith is belief in **tawhid**, which means the oneness and unity of Allah. It is summed up very well in almost the last chapter of the Qur'an:

> 'Say: He is Allah, the One;
> Allah, the Eternal, the Absolute;
> He begetteth not, nor is He begotten;
> And there is none like unto Him.'

Sura 112, translated by S. Mahmood

Allahu Akbar (The Takbir), 'Allah is the ▲ Greatest'.

If there is only one God, then he alone is the creator of all that exists, but was not himself created, he is 'The Eternal'. If there is only one God, then he alone is all-powerful and in control of the universe, he is 'The Almighty', 'The Omnipotent'.

Tawhid has some far-reaching implications in Islam.

- Muslims should worship Allah alone; no one else and nothing else is worthy. No other being should be associated with Allah. Idolatry is worshipping something less than God, and it is strictly forbidden. This sin of idolatry is called **shirk**, and is regarded by Muslims as the worst of all sins.
- A Muslim's whole life should be lived for Allah alone. Islam gives rules to govern all aspects of one's life.
- If there is only one God, there should be only one religion. Islam is seen as the best religion for the whole world.
- Those who believe in the oneness of Allah should be united together in their religion. Islam emphasises the unity of the **Ummah**, the world-wide Islamic community. (See also pp.86–87.)
- Belief in the oneness of Allah who created all humankind also teaches Muslims to regard all human beings as being created equal by God, irrespective of race, colour, language, gender, intelligence, wealth or social standing.
- Belief in one creator gives a sense of oneness with all creation. Therefore Muslims should respect other human beings, animals and natural resources. In particular, there is a sense of belonging to all humanity, because of the belief that all human beings were created from 'a single soul' (Qur'an 4:1) – that we all descended from Adam, the first human being. Muslims believe that God treats everyone equally, and so should we. Muslims believe that Allah made human beings with rational intelligence and free will so that they could take responsibility for the rest of creation, just as Adam did. Islam speaks of humanity as **khalifah**, that is, Allah's representatives on earth and custodians of creation on his behalf.
- If there is only one God, then he must be totally in control. (See **qadar**, that follows.)

▲ Muslims believe that God is the creator of all that exists.

THE SIXTH ARTICLE OF FAITH?

Another implication of Tawhid is the Muslim belief in **qadar**, which is so important in Islam that it is sometimes regarded as the sixth Article of Faith. This is the belief in predestination, or that God controls our destinies. Muslims believe that God is all-powerful, he is in control of his creation and ordains everything that happens. Nothing happens unless it is the will of Allah. Muslims frequently say 'Insha Allah', meaning 'If Allah is willing', showing their recognition of his power and acceptance of his will for them. Remember that a Muslim is someone who *submits* to the will of Allah in all things.

There is a danger that this belief in predestination could lead to fatalism – the view that we do not need to bother, i.e. what will be will be. Islam teaches against this. There is a Hadith story about the Prophet and one of his Companions. They stopped on their journey and dismounted their camels. Muhammad wanted to tie up the camels, but his Companion asked why they

needed to, since the camels were in God's hands. The Prophet's reply was that they should tie up the camels first and then leave them in God's hands. So, belief in al-qadar does not mean that human beings should just sit back and do nothing. It means rather that they should work with God, but that God has foreknowledge of what will happen.

Why then, you may ask, does God let terrible things happen to people, if he is all-powerful and knows what will happen? Muslims would say that God knows what is best for us, even if we do not realise it ourselves at the time. God created suffering as well as happiness, but there is a purpose in suffering.

Islam insists that we have free will to choose right or wrong, and we are therefore responsible for our own sins, but that God knows us so well that he knows how we will choose. They believe that God has a good purpose and destiny for each person, which we can go along with, or we can reject God's way for us.

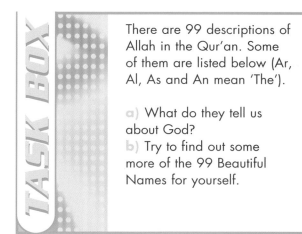

TASK BOX

There are 99 descriptions of Allah in the Qur'an. Some of them are listed below (Ar, Al, As and An mean 'The').

a) What do they tell us about God?
b) Try to find out some more of the 99 Beautiful Names for yourself.

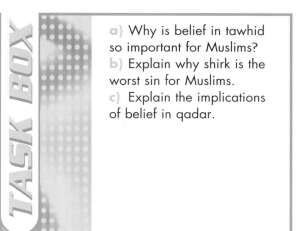

TASK BOX

a) Why is belief in tawhid so important for Muslims?
b) Explain why shirk is the worst sin for Muslims.
c) Explain the implications of belief in qadar.

Some of the 99 Beautiful Names	
Ar-Rahman	The Merciful
Ar-Rahīm	The Compassionate
Al-Malik	The One Who Rules
As-Salām	The Peace
Al-'Azīz	The Almighty/Powerful
Al-Khāliq	The Creator
Al-Hakam	The Judge
Al-Halīm	The Patient
Al-Karīm	The Generous
Al-Mujīb	The One Who Answers
Al-Mumīt	The Bringer of Death
As-Samad	The Perfect/Eternal
An-Nūr	The Light
Ar-Rashīd	The Guide

TEST YOURSELF

1 What are the five most important things for a Muslim to believe in?
2 What are the words of the Shahada?
3 What is the worst sin in Islam?
4 What is tawhid?
5 To whom do the 99 Beautiful Names refer?

WHAT DO MUSLIMS BELIEVE ABOUT ANGELS?

Islam teaches that Allah is the only spiritual being to be worshipped, but that there are other supernatural beings, said to be created from light, called angels. These are the heavenly servants of Allah. Unlike human beings, the angels have no free will of their own, and are therefore sinless.

Muhammad said these angels surround us at all times and will present a full report on us after death. It is believed that two angels watch over each one of us and come to the grave to take charge of our soul until the Day of Resurrection: one to report on our good deeds, and the other to report on the bad.

In the following verses of the Qur'an, the two archangels, Gabriel (Jebreel) and Michael are named. Gabriel is also referred to in the Qur'an as the holy spirit (which must not be confused with the Christian idea of God, the Holy Spirit). Islam teaches that Gabriel brought Allah's revelations to the Prophets and, in particular, the Qur'an to Muhammad.

> Say (O Muhammad, to mankind): Who is an enemy to Gabriel! For he it is who hath revealed (this Scripture) to thy heart by Allah's leave, confirming that which was (revealed) before it, and a guidance and glad tidings to believers;
>
> Who is an enemy to Allah, and His angels and His messengers, and Gabriel and Michael! Then, lo! Allah (Himself) is an enemy to the disbelievers.
>
> *Qur'an 2:97–98 (Pickthall)*

▲ This scene, showing winged angels, is taken from an Islamic carpet (from India, seventeenth century). It is likely that the angel in the centre is Jebreel (Gabriel).

Although Islam teaches that it is wrong to depict living creatures, not all Muslim artists have followed this teaching. The reason why Islam forbids it is that Muhammad recalled Muslims to the worship of the one God, Allah, from the worship of idols. Idolatry is the worst sin in Islam and anything that could lead to it is therefore avoided. At least the artist has left the faces blank.

Another archangel, Izrail, is the 'angel of death'; and the fourth, Israfil, will blow the trumpet to herald the Last Day. We also read of Iblis, the fallen angel. This is Islam's name for the Devil or Satan. In the creation story, we read this:

> And when We said unto the angels: Prostrate yourselves before Adam, they fell prostrate, all save Iblis. He demurred through pride, and so became a disbeliever.
>
> *Qur'an 2:34 (Pickthall)*

(Note that 'We' refers to Allah. Like the 'royal we', it refers to only one.)

TEST YOURSELF

A B C According to Muslim belief:

1 What are angels?
2 Which archangel revealed the Qur'an to Muhammad?
3 Name another of the four archangels.
4 Why do people have two angels watching over them?
5 Which fallen angel became Satan?

WHICH HOLY BOOKS DO MUSLIMS BELIEVE IN?

▲ Jewish Torah scrolls

▲ A Christian Bible opened at the beginning of the New Testament.

Muslims believe that, through the ages, Allah has revealed his truth through his prophets, and that this has been written down in holy books. They believe that Ibrahim (Abraham) brought a book, which is now lost. They accept the Jewish Scriptures: the **Tawrah** brought by Musa (the Torah of Moses), and the **Zabur** of Dawud (the Psalms of David). They also believe in the **Injil** of Isa (the Gospel brought by Jesus). Jews and Christians are therefore known as People of the Book. They believe that Allah sent other holy books to other people of the world, which are not named in the Qur'an.

Muslims believe that most of these revelations are now lost. The others they consider to be corrupted, i.e. Allah's words became mixed up with human interpretations, and there is now no means of knowing what is true. Therefore, although they believe that Allah inspired both Judaism and Christianity, they do not accept everything that their Scriptures say. Muslims also believe that Allah sent books at certain times in history to particular people. So his rules for the Jews, for example, do not necessarily apply to all people for all time.

So it was necessary for Allah to send down a further revelation: the Holy Qur'an. Islam teaches that this book contains the complete and uncorrupted words of Allah for all people, everywhere, in all ages. They believe the Qur'an is the timeless truth from Allah to humanity.

> Allah hath revealed the Scripture with the truth.
>
> *Qur'an 2:176*
>
> Those unto whom We have given the Scripture, who read it with the right reading, those believe in it. And whoso disbelieveth in it, those are they who are the losers.
>
> *Qur'an 2:121 (Pickthall)*

WHICH PROPHETS DO MUSLIMS BELIEVE IN?

> Say (O Muslims): We believe in Allah and that which is revealed unto us and that which was revealed unto Abraham, and Ishmael, and Isaac, and Jacob, and the tribes, and that which Moses and Jesus received, and that which the Prophets received from their Lord.
>
> *Qur'an 2:136 (Pickthall)*

A prophet is someone through whom God speaks. Muslim tradition says there have been 124,000 prophets in all. The Qur'an itself names 25 prophets, most of whom are found in the Bible (see selected examples in the box on the following page). Whenever Muslims mention one of them, they say 'Peace be upon him' (PBUH).

Qur'anic Name	Biblical Name
Adam	Adam
Nuh	Noah
Ibrahim	Abraham
Isma'il	Ishmael
Ishaq	Isaac
Yusuf	Joseph
Musa	Moses
Dawud	David
Sulayman	Solomon
Yunus	Jonah
Yahya	John
Isa	Jesus
Muhammad	

Nabi is the word used for most of these prophets; **rasul** usually describes a prophet who has brought a holy book, and **risala** means prophecy. Prophets associated with a holy book are known as the Messengers of Allah, i.e. Ibrahim, Musa, Dawud, Isa and Muhammad. So, belief in prophethood is closely linked with the third Article of Faith: belief in holy books.

The prophets are an important link between God and humankind. Muslims believe that Allah revealed through them what he is like and how he wants people to live in order to gain eternal happiness in the afterlife. Islam teaches that, since all true prophets were inspired by Allah, they all brought the same basic truth: that there is only one God, and that he will punish the wicked and reward the good. Some people believed these prophets, but there were always those who rejected them, and their messages were lost or distorted.

Notice that Islam recognises Jesus (called Isa) as a prophet: he is mentioned in 15 chapters of the Qur'an and in 93 verses. Like Christianity, Islam believes in the miraculous virgin birth of Jesus to Mary:

▲ A Christian image of Mary and Jesus from St Sophia's in Istanbul, Turkey.

But Islam does not believe that Jesus really died on the cross, and therefore does not believe in the resurrection. However, it does believe in his ascension into heaven.

Muslims regard Jesus as sinless but still human – not divine. They call him 'son of Mary' – not 'Son of God' because of their firm belief in the oneness of Allah. They are unable to accept any suggestion that God has a son, or that he is three persons, whereas Christians speak of the 'three persons' of the Trinity. (Christians believe that the One God has revealed himself in three roles: as Father, Son and Holy Spirit.)

> She said: 'How can I have a boy when no human being has ever touched me, nor am I a loose-living woman?' He said: 'Thus your Lord has said: "It is a simple matter for Me [to do]. We will make him as a sign for mankind and as a mercy from Ourself. It is a matter that has been decided."'
>
> *Qur'an 19:20–21 (The Qur'an, Basic Teachings, p.118)*

> Those who say that God is Christ, the son of Mary, have disbelieved. Christ (himself) said: 'Children of Israel, serve God [who is] my Lord as well as your Lord.' … Those who say: 'God is the third of three', have disbelieved. There is no deity except God Alone.
>
> *Qur'an 5:72–3 from The Qur'an, Basic Teachings pp. 120–121*

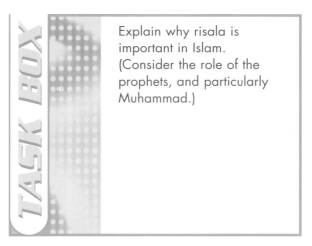

TASK BOX

Explain why risala is important in Islam.
(Consider the role of the prophets, and particularly Muhammad.)

There are many points of similarity between these two religions, such as in their ethical teachings and belief in the Day of Judgement; but Muslims regard Islam as a correction and completion of Christianity.

For Muslims, Muhammad is Allah's last prophet, known as the 'Seal of the Prophets' (33:40), who brought the final message that has been preserved intact in the Qur'an. This is the final and complete message from Allah to humanity. Muslims therefore strongly deny any claims to prophethood that have been made since the time of Muhammad.

TEST YOURSELF

1 Name the five prophets who were rasuls/messengers of Allah.
2 How many prophets are named in the Qur'an?
3 Who was the first of these?
4 What does 'PBUH' stand for, and when is it used?
5 What is the Arabic name for Jesus?
6 Do Muslims believe in the virgin birth of Jesus?
7 Do Muslims believe that Jesus was the Son of God?
8 Who is called the Seal of the Prophets and what does it mean?

WHAT DO MUSLIMS BELIEVE ABOUT LIFE AFTER DEATH?

Belief in life after death (**akhirah**) is fundamental to Islam. The Qur'an is full of warnings to disbelievers about the doom awaiting them after death, as well as of promises of good things for those who submit to Allah. The Hadith, too, contain much teaching on this important matter.

Muslims believe that this life is only a short part of our existence. This is our chance to live good lives, as Allah intended, or to turn our backs on Allah and his laws. They believe that after death we shall have to answer for the way we have used our lives, and this will affect our eternal destinies.

Muhammad taught that, at death, souls are questioned by two angels who ask: 'Who is your Lord?' 'What is your religion?' and 'Who is that man who was sent amongst you?', i.e. the Prophet (*Selection from Hadith*, p.176). Those who know that Allah is the only God and that Muhammad is his Prophet remain in comfort until the Day of Resurrection. The rest are kept in great discomfort.

> Uthman reported that when the Holy Prophet (peace and blessings of Allah be upon him) had completed the burial of the dead he stood on his grave and said: Seek forgiveness for your brother and beseech (Allah) for his steadfastness (in the hour of his trial) for now he is being questioned.
>
> *Abu Dawud; Selection from Hadith, No.340, p.175*

Islam teaches that, at the Last Day, the end of the world will come. Then everyone will be raised up and each individual will be judged by Allah himself. Everyone will be sorry for the wrong they have done, and for not doing more good with their lives. People will be judged not only on their deeds but also on their faith. Believers will have their sins forgiven and will go to heaven, for Allah is merciful and compassionate; but disbelievers will go to hell. They had their chance on earth to turn to Allah, and now it is too late. Heaven and hell are described in the Qur'an as physical states: the one, like a wonderful garden, where people will be young again and able to enjoy all its pleasures; the other, like a scorching fire that is never put out.

> The unbelievers of the People of the Book and the idolaters shall be in the Fire of Gehenna, therein dwelling forever; those are the worst of creatures.
> But those who believe, and do righteous deeds, those are the best of creatures; their recompense is with their Lord – Gardens of Eden, underneath which rivers flow, therein dwelling for ever and ever. God is well-pleased with them, and they are well-pleased with Him; that is for him who fears his Lord.
>
> *Qur'an 98:5–8 (Arberry)*

And finally, this surah describes the end of the world, before the Day of Judgement.

> **The Splitting**
> In the Name of God, the Merciful, the Compassionate.
>   When heaven is split open,
>   when the stars are scattered,
>   when the seas swarm over,
>   when the tombs are overthrown,
> then a soul shall know its works, the former and the latter.
>
> O Man! What deceived thee as to thy generous Lord who created thee and shaped thee and wrought thee in symmetry
>   and composed thee after what form He would?
>   No indeed; but you cry lies to the Doom;
>   yet there are over you watchers
>   noble, writers
>   who know whatever you do.
>
>   Surely the pious shall be in bliss,
> and the libertines shall be in a fiery furnace
>   roasting therein on the Day of Doom,
>   nor shall they ever be absent from it.
>
> And what shall teach thee what is the Day of Doom?
> Again, what shall teach thee what is the Day of Doom?
> A day when no soul shall possess aught to succour another soul;
>   that day the Command shall belong unto God.
>
> *Qur'an 82 (Arberry)*

WEBLINKS

- www.al-quran.org.uk (for Qu'ranic text and wordsearch)
- www.islamicity.com (under 'Mosque and Religions', for the Most Beautiful Names of Allah)
- www.islam4kids.com (e.g. on Tawhid – website for Muslim children, requires Acrobat Reader)
- www.islam101.com (for Qur'an, Allah)

---

1 a) Describe the Qur'an for someone who knows nothing about it.

b) Explain as fully as possible why the Qur'an is so important to Muslims.

c) Do you think a holy book should be treated differently from any other book?
Give reasons to support your answer and show that you have thought about different points of view. You must refer to Islam in your answer.

2 a) Describe what the Qur'an teaches about the Last Day, Heaven and Hell.

b) Explain how belief in the afterlife has a strong influence on Muslims' earthly lives.

c) 'This life is more important than the next.'
Do you agree? Give reasons to support your answer and show that you have thought about different points of view. You must refer to Islam in your answer.

(Third part of question taken from Religious Studies B, Paper 1 June 2003 OCR.)

Assignment

5

KEY WORDS

Id Mubarak: 'Happy Festival' – the festival greeting.
Id-ul-Fitr: Festival of Fast Breaking.
iftar: breakfast – it literally breaks the fast.
khutbah: the Friday sermon.
Laylat-ul-Qadr: the Night of Power, when Muhammad is said to have received the first revelation of the Qur'an, commemorated annually in Islam.
lunar: to do with the moon – the Muslim calendar is based on lunar months.
Ramadan: the month of fasting.
riba: charging interest on loans of money.
sadaqah: voluntary charity.
Salat al-Id: festival prayer session.
sawm: Arabic for fasting – the Ramadan fast is one of the pillars of Islam.
zakah: charity tax – a pillar of Islam, 2½ per cent of a Muslim's wealth is given away.
Zakat-ul-Fitr: festival charity – in addition to zakah, the Third Pillar of Islam.

KEY QUESTION

How do Muslims keep Ramadan and why is fasting important to them?

Ibn Umar reported that the people saw the new moon (of Ramadan). So I informed the Messenger of Allah (peace and blessings of Allah be upon him) that I had seen the new moon. Upon this the Holy Prophet observed fasting and ordered the people to observe the fasts of Ramadan.

Sunan Abu Dawud; Selection of Hadith, No.55

WHY DO MUSLIMS FAST DURING RAMADAN?

Ramadan is the ninth month of the Islamic calendar. It was during this month that Muhammad received his first revelation of the Qur'an. For this reason, it is a special month for Muslims, which they commemorate by fasting (called **sawm**). Their fasts entail going without food and drink during the daylight hours of every day of the month. Muslims also pay extra attention to the Qur'an during this month; many read it right through from beginning to end.

There are two main reasons why Muslims fast. The first is that it is the Fourth Pillar of Islam (and therefore an obligatory duty and act of worship) commanded for them by Allah in the Qur'an:

O ye who believe! Fasting is prescribed for you, even as it was prescribed for those before you, that you may ward off [evil].

Qur'an 2:183 (Pickthall)

The second reason is that Muhammad himself set them the example of fasting:

RAMADAN

Day	Fast starts	Sunrise	Fast ends	Day	Fast starts	Sunrise	Fast ends
Mon 27/10	04:44	06:43	16:45	Mon 10/11	05:05	07:08	16:21
Tue 28/10	04:45	06:45	16:43	Tue 11/11	05:07	07:09	16:19
Wed 29/10	04:47	06:46	16:42	Wed 12/11	05:08	07:11	16:18
Thu 30/10	04:48	06:48	16:40	Thu 13/11	05:10	07:13	16:16
Fri 31/10	04:50	06:50	16:38	Fri 14/11	05:11	07:15	16:15
Sat 01/11	04:52	06:52	16:36	Sat 15/11	05:13	07:16	16:14
Sun 02/11	04:53	06:53	16:34	Sun 16/11	05:14	07:18	16:12
Mon 03/11	04:55	06:55	16:32	Mon 17/11	05:15	07:20	16:11
Tue 04/11	04:56	06:57	16:31	Tue 18/11	05:17	07:21	16:10
Wed 05/11	04:58	06:59	16:29	Wed 19/11	05:18	07:23	16:08
Thu 06/11	04:59	07:01	16:27	Thu 20/11	05:19	07:25	16:07
Fri 07/11	05:01	07:02	16:26	Fri 21/11	05:21	07:26	16:06
Sat 08/11	05:02	07:04	16:24	Sat 22/11	05:22	07:28	16:05
Sun 09/11	05:04	07:06	16:22	Sun 23/11	05:24	07:30	16:04

▲ An example of a Ramadan timetable.

Muslims who are not expected to fast.

WHO SHOULD FAST?

Any Muslim who is capable of fasting should do so; but no one should endanger life or health because of it. Consequently, women who are menstruating, pregnant, or breast-feeding should not fast. Nor should people who are ill and could make themselves worse by fasting.

Muslim soldiers, or people on long journeys, will need to keep up their strength and so they are also excused from fasting. These people should try to make up the fast-days they have missed, at another time. If they cannot do this, then they should give the cost of two meals to the poor, for each fast-day they miss, if they can afford to do so.

Elderly people are not expected to fast, but they too are asked to feed the poor instead, if they can afford it.

Young children will gradually be introduced to fasting, perhaps for just half a day at first. Once they reach the age of puberty, they will have to do the same fasts as the adults. This is often taken to apply from 12 years old.

Lastly, the insane are not required to fast. They would not understand what was going on, and would not be able to gain any spiritual benefit from this religious duty, but would simply be given unnecessary suffering.

▲ Many Muslims spend more time reading the Qur'an during Ramadan. These men are in Indonesia.

WHEN IS THE FAST?

Fasting goes on every day of the month of Ramadan (29/30 days). The Muslim calendar is based on the moon, and the sighting of the new moon marks the beginning of each new month. The **lunar** year is about 11 days shorter than the Western year (which is based on the sun), so the Muslim months rotate backwards, each year, through the seasons. Fasting takes place during daylight hours, from dawn (about two hours before sunrise) until sunset. When Ramadan falls in summer, the days can be very long in some countries, and the fasting is particularly demanding. (Muslims in the 'Lands of the midnight sun' have a problem because, in mid-summer, there is no night-time! They usually fast from 6 a.m. to 6 p.m.)

▲ Muslim months begin with the sighting of the new moon. Here there is rejoicing at the end of the month of Ramadan.

▲ A cannon is fired in Qatar to signal that the fast is over for the day.

WHAT IS IT LIKE TO FAST?

A typical fast-day begins very early in the morning, because Muslims get up to have something to drink and something nourishing to eat before the fast begins. In the winter, when nights are long, this early morning meal is often quite substantial. But in the summer, it might have to be eaten only a few hours after finishing the night meal, and will therefore be quite light. High-energy foods are usually eaten, such as yoghurt, cheese and honey. Spicy foods are avoided, because they make people extra thirsty.

In many Muslim countries, people are woken up in time for this meal by drum-beaters or by cannon-fire. In non-Muslim countries, they follow the timetables issued by the mosques, and have to rely on their own alarm clocks to wake them.

(Look again at the timetable on page 54, for typical fasting hours during Ramadan in the UK.)

During the day, it will be difficult for Muslims who are fasting to continue with their normal work, particularly anything strenuous; the whole pace of life slows down in Muslim countries. It is more difficult, of course, in non-Muslim countries, if no allowance is made. The following advice is given to teachers in Britain:

Children who are fasting may feel weak and tired during the day, especially in the afternoon. Strenuous physical exercise may make them feel worse ... Those children who go swimming may be concerned about swallowing water – strictly speaking this would be breaking the fast – so they will spit it out.

Teachers should avoid giving the impression that fasting is 'a nuisance, disruptive to school routine and work', but should view it as something positive. They must accept that a child's attitudes, behaviour and performance may in some cases be affected, but that these changes are purely temporary. They should acknowledge their acceptance of fasting by showing interest and asking questions about fasting routines. They should accept that Britain is a multi-religious and multi-cultural society; tolerance and respect should be given to the other's faith and culture.

The Muslim Guide, p.49

PERSPECTIVES

Nadia, a young Muslim girl, describes her difficulties in keeping the fast (of over 18 hours) while at school in Britain. We take up the story at morning break.

As Fouzia had told most of my friends that I was fasting, I didn't expect anybody to offer me any crisps but I received exactly the opposite. Nearly all my friends offered me something, but I refused ...

'Is it easy to fast?' asked Shanie.

'The answer is No, but I try my best to keep faith in God and I shall hopefully complete today's fast.'[...] Jane and I started walking around the playground. She had some sweets and was kind enough not to offer me any. Walking about, Jane asked me, 'Don't you get thirsty or hungry?'

'Of course I do, but I'm not very hungry yet, my mouth is dry though.'

'Shall we go to the cloakroom?' Jane suggested.

'Good idea!' I exclaimed. We went to the cloakroom. Jane had a drink but I could only rinse my mouth. A couple of minutes later we went back to class. We had maths till quarter past twelve. Then it was lunchtime. I could see people lining up for school lunch.

Hayley asked me, 'Are you having packed lunch or school lunch?'

'Neither', I replied, 'because I am fasting and I can't eat or drink anything till twenty past nine in the evening, precisely nine hours from now.' We played together for a while until the whistle went for packed lunch people, so I played with Fouzia and other friends who had finished their lunch. As we were playing a first year girl came up to me and started teasing me ...

'Would you like some cream cakes or jam doughnuts, maybe some chocolates, you might like some currant buns', she began. 'I think sweets and crisps are nice, too', she finished. I was really getting angry. I don't know how people could be so ignorant.

Eid Mubarak, pp.12–14

Nadia Bakhsh was only ten years old when she wrote her book *Eid Mubarak*, from which this passage is taken. Despite the difficulties described here, she says that she enjoyed her first fast so much that she wanted everyone to know what it felt like for a child to fast.

Past my mid-forties and an Englishman accustomed to eating more than necessary and smoking like a chimney, I approached Ramadan with a fast growing apprehension. ... I had ideas of going to Morocco to escape the temptations of England but it was not the Will of Allah. In answer to my prayers for help, I remained in England and taught a group of Muslim students. From them I learned to fast. From Allah I was given strength to fulfil both my spiritual and teaching obligations without great distress. On the contrary, at the permitted times for eating, after sunset and at dawn, Muslims make this a time for close and kindly relationships. My next Ramadan? I am apprehensive but I now know the energy and help to expect from worship – it is the Reward of Ramadan.

The Muslim Guide, p.27

As the above passage suggests, fasting can be even more difficult for Western converts to Islam who have not been brought up to do it.

Not only must Muslims give up food and drink, but also sexual relations and smoking (during daylight hours). If you have ever known someone trying to give up smoking, you will appreciate how difficult this can be.

Muslims are also supposed to give up bad thoughts and wrong-doings during Ramadan. Not that these things are excusable at any time, but this special month reminds Muslims to be particularly careful about living up to the high moral standards of their religion. Also, because all Muslims are fasting together, there is a greater sense of comradeship than at some other times, and therefore unpleasantness to one another is less likely.

WHAT ELSE DO MUSLIMS DO DURING RAMADAN?

This special month is also a chance to give more attention to prayer and the reading of the Qur'an. Many Muslims perform an extra prayer with either eight or 20 rak'ahs, after the night prayer. Mosques arrange extra opportunities for people to learn about their religion, as is shown by the programme of daily lectures throughout Ramadan, at the London Central Mosque.

Many Muslims make a special effort to attend congregational prayers at the mosque each day – not just on Fridays. Food is provided to break the fast for those who attend the sunset prayer. Some Muslims stay at the mosque for the last ten days of the month, during which **Laylat-ul-Qadr** is celebrated. The Night of Power is normally accepted to have been on the 27th of the month, but tradition says that it was at least during these last ten days. Muslims who do this religious retreat spend the time in religious study, prayer and meditation.

TASK BOX

a) Explain why Muslims usually get up early on fast days.

b) Explain why it is difficult for Muslims to fast in non-Muslim countries.

c) Why do you think it is likely to be more difficult for women to fast than men?

TEST YOURSELF

1 What else do Muslims do during Ramadan apart from give things up?

2 When is the holiest part of the month?

3 What do some Muslims do during this part of the month?

▲ A Turkish family shares a meal together at the end of a day in Ramadan.

Although no food may be eaten during the day, food is still bought and sold, and women have to prepare food for the night-time. Like the preparations for any celebration, this can be an exhausting time for them, which continues throughout the month.

As each day's fast draws to its close, Muslims feel excited, proud of their endurance, and very hungry and thirsty. They wait for the announcement on television or radio, or by means of a call from the minaret, that sunset has come. Then they break their fast with **iftar** (breakfast). They eat very little at first, to get their digestive systems gradually used to food again. They will drink a glass of water, or a sweet drink to quench their thirst and restore some of their energy. It is traditional to eat sweet dates, or the popular 'stars of the moon', which are dried apricots that have soaked all day in sugar water.

The **Maghrib** prayer (the salah for sunset) is said before the main meal is eaten. Sometimes this meal is left until late at night, and may take the form of an elaborate dinner party. Those who

have kept the fast together throughout the day now celebrate together at night. The poor are given food or invited to share a meal, so that they too can enjoy the pleasures of Ramadan. At the London Central Mosque, for example, people donate money to provide a banquet every night during Ramadan for 2000 lonely, single or needy Muslims. Children too, in Muslim countries, enter into the party spirit. They go round the streets with candle-lit lanterns, singing songs at people's doors and being rewarded with money and sweets.

Non-Muslims sometimes think it is strange that Muslims should go without food all day, and then make up for it at night. But it is the discipline of it which is important, rather than the fact of going without. Islam does not teach people to go to extremes; it knows our body's needs, and does not ask more than is humanly possible or advisable. As with the case of those who are excused fasting, the Qur'an says: 'He (Allah) desireth not hardship for you' (2:185).

▲ Supermarkets are busy in Muslim countries during Ramadan as people prepare for the evening meal. This is in Amman, in Jordan.

People enjoy the food all the more because they have gone without it earlier. They join in the celebrations because they feel they have deserved them. But what about those Muslims who did not manage to keep the fast? Some may have broken it by accident, such as swallowing a mouthful of water while in the shower, or eating a sweet from a friend without thinking. They can make up for this if they wish with an extra day's fast after the Festival. It is much more serious when Muslims give way to temptation and break the fast on purpose. To make up for this, they should fast for 60 consecutive days. If their health will not permit this, then they can pay for a meal for 60 poor people.

In any religious community, there are always some who are non-practising. But, in Muslim countries, there is a lot of social pressure on everyone to fast, even if they do not keep other religious rules. Even in Britain, where Muslims are a minority in a secular society, between 75 and 80 per cent of them keep Ramadan.

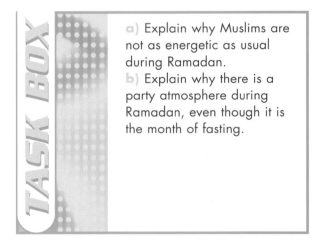

TASK BOX

a) Explain why Muslims are not as energetic as usual during Ramadan.

b) Explain why there is a party atmosphere during Ramadan, even though it is the month of fasting.

HOW DO MUSLIMS BENEFIT FROM FASTING?

You may be asked the purpose of **sawm.** This can include both the reasons for fasting and its benefits. The reasons why Muslims fast are given at the beginning of this chapter but on the following page are some of the benefits that Muslims may gain from fasting.

1 There is a feeling of togetherness, as all Muslims, rich and poor, fulfil the same demands of the fast and then share their food together at night.

> An Arab businessman, who had arrived at the mosque in a chauffeur-driven blue Rolls-Royce and was sitting in obvious discomfort while listening to the lesson from the imam before the sunset prayer, said: 'When you see the wealthy, the powerful and the famous sitting on the carpeted floor next to the poor and eating the same food, you see the true spirit of equality which Islam has brought to mankind.'
>
> *The Independent, 2 May 1988*

2 The rich gain a better understanding of what it must be like for the poor who cannot always eat when they want to. This should make them more generous towards them.

> In fasting they have the chance to share some of the anguish of hunger and poverty experienced by the distressed and destitute of the world. From this experience, they learn to be increasingly grateful and generous.
>
> *The Muslim Guide, p.26*

3 Muslims will learn to appreciate all the good things they have each day, and to thank Allah for them, instead of just taking them for granted.

4 They will learn self-control.

> Over-indulgence in eating, drinking and marital relations makes one the slave of desires and habits. It is believed that fasting frees one from this slavery. The purpose of fasting in Islam is to control passions and thus making one a person of good deeds and intentions.
>
> *From Islam, Sawm and Hajj*

5 They will learn how to endure hardships.

> Just as we might go to the dentist and put up with a certain amount of suffering because we know it is necessary for our health and well-being, so the Muslim regards Ramadan. Putting up with a small amount of hardship teaches a person to have patience and perseverance and develops the qualities of courage and steadfastness in the face of difficulties.
>
> *Ramadan and Id-ul-Fitr, p.13*

6 Throughout the month, they will be reminded constantly of the importance of worshipping Allah, not just for this life, but for eternity.

> Salman Al-Farisi reported that the Messenger of Allah (peace and blessings of Allah be upon him) addressed us on the last day of Sha'ban and said: 'O people, a great and blessed month is near at hand. … It is the month of endurance and the reward of endurance is Paradise.'
>
> *Shu'ab Al-Iman; Selection from Hadith, No.61, pp.34–5*

TASK BOX

On six cards, briefly write out the six benefits of fasting.

Arrange them in order, putting the one you think is most important first.

Compare your order with a partner's and, through discussion, come to an agreed order.

Join with another pair and come to an agreed order for the four of you.

Each group should then read out their first and last reasons as the teacher keeps the score. Be prepared to defend your decisions.

How is Id-ul-Fitr celebrated at the end of Ramadan?

WHEN IS ID-UL-FITR?

'Is it Id? Is it Id tomorrow?' I asked anxiously.
'We don't know yet,' my mum said. My dad then had a good idea.

'I'll phone the Islamic Cultural Centre (Regents Park Mosque, London). They often have the latest information.' My dad phoned but it was engaged ... It took some time to get to sleep but I eventually did. It was difficult to sleep because of the excitement of Id, whether it was on or not. I woke up early and went downstairs to see if there were any Id cards. There were a few so I took them upstairs to my parents who opened them. One of the envelopes contained £5. It was from Pakistan. The money was for me as an idi from my grandmum. I displayed all the cards on the mantelpiece.

I asked my mum and dad, 'Is it Id? Is it Id today? Please tell me!'

My mum spoke next, 'We phoned at 3 o'clock this morning, and found out it's Id!'

'Hooray! Hooray!' I was so pleased. 'Id Mubarak,' I said to both my mum and dad.

Eid Mubarak, pp.24 and 27

Imagine going to bed on what you thought was Christmas Eve, not knowing for sure if it really would be Christmas the next day! Yet that is the uncertainty Muslims have to live with at Id-ul-Fitr. Each Islamic month begins at new moon. Islamic calendars are based on the probable visibility of the new moon by the naked eye; but festivals cannot be observed until the new moon is *actually* seen by at least two witnesses. Calendars therefore include the proviso 'Subject to the sighting of the moon'.

In Muslim countries, people usually stay up at the end of Ramadan, and when they see the new moon of the month of Shawwal, there is great rejoicing. Cannon-fire used to boom out the message that the month of fasting had finished and the festival had begun. Now it is more usual for it to be announced on the radio and television. In the West, a cloudy sky frequently obscures the moon, so Muslims here have to rely on the message coming through to their centres from Muslim countries like Morocco (which is nearest to Britain).

Id-ul-Fitr means 'Festival of Fast Breaking'. It is the most popular festival of all, especially with the children who get lots of presents, money, sweets and new clothes. The intensity of the whole month of fasting has been leading up to this. The preparations involve all the trappings we associate with celebrations (or most of them): decorating the house, sending cards, buying and wrappings gifts, wearing our best clothes, and preparing special food. (Westerners might notice the absence of alcohol.)

▲ Islamic greetings cards. They wish people '**Id Mubarak**' which means a 'Blessed' or 'Happy Festival'.

▲ Muslim children celebrating Id-ul-Fitr.

Remembering that this is a religious festival, families attend mosque in the morning for special Id prayers. So many people go that extra space has to be found, often outside, where sheets or mats are laid down on the ground. At some big centres it is also necessary for a number of services to be held in relay, as shown by these five morning services held at the London Central Mosque:

1st Prayer	6.00 a.m.
2nd Prayer	7.30 a.m.
3rd Prayer	9.00 a.m.
4th Prayer	10.00 a.m.
5th Prayer	11.00 a.m.

When the prayers are over, the parties begin. Friends and families get together, call on one another and forget old quarrels. This should be a time of *peace* (the meaning of 'Islam'). Birthdays that fall during Ramadan are celebrated at Id-ul-Fitr; and a good number of weddings take place on Id days. During all these family celebrations, many Muslims also remember relatives who have died, and visit their graves.

Muhammad called Id-ul-Fitr the 'Day of Reward', coming as it does after the trials of Ramadan. Muslims thank Allah for giving them the strength to endure the fast. Now they can relax and enjoy all the good things that Allah has given them. In Muslim countries, this is a national holiday of between two and four days long. In Western countries, Muslims take a day off work or school.

Yet another name for Id-ul-Fitr is the 'Festival of Charity' because steps are taken to make sure that the poor, too, can enjoy good food at this time. Every Muslim who can afford it pays **Zakat-ul-Fitr**. This special religious tax for the Id is the cost of a meal per head. This charity should be paid before the Id prayer, showing that there are times when caring for others takes priority even over prayer. Usually, it is paid several days beforehand so that it can be distributed in good time for the festival. (See the photo on page 67.)

Working in pairs, read these instructions for Id day, issued by the London Central Mosque. Each write down five questions beginning with 'Why … ?' based on this information. Then take turns to ask your partner your questions.

'In order to derive the maximum benefit from the great day of thanksgiving and rejoicing that is Id-ul-Fitr and in order that the Salat should be conducted in as serene and orderly manner as possible, we kindly request worshippers to observe the following instructions.

- Please perform Wudu before coming to the Mosque.
- All worshippers are requested to observe proper Islamic dress on this occasion in particular and at all times. Ladies are reminded that Islamic dress requires them to cover their body with the exception of the face and hands. Transparent clothing is not allowed.
- On reaching the mosque, observe Police parking instructions. Come in time and park away from the mosque to avoid congestion. No parking is allowed on the mosque premises. Cars parked in Park Road or Hanover Gate are at risk of being removed by the Police.
- Please follow the signs at the mosque in order to avoid congestion.
- A one-way system has been devised where worshippers are required to enter the Prayer Halls by the main gates and leave by the other exits indicated.
- Ladies are particularly requested to observe the one-way system as facilities are inadequate for large numbers at the mosque.
- Please use the polythene bags provided to keep your shoes with you and discard the bags together with other litter in the bins provided. Keep the mosque premises clean.
- Attendants are available for any assistance. Please help them to help you.
- Children lost in the crowd must be reported to the Lost and Found Centre Point located underneath the flats.
- Please remember that the **Khutbah** in Arabic and English is part of **Salat al–Id** and worshippers should sit quietly until the Khutbah is complete. Please do not talk during the Khutbah as this invalidates the Prayers.
- When you have finished the Id prayer, please leave the premises as quickly as possible for the next session of worshippers.

May Allah accept your Prayer and grant you all the blessings of Id.'

▲ Muslims gathered outside the London Central Mosque at Id-ul-Fitr.

TEST YOURSELF

A B C

1 Give the three English titles for Id-ul-Fitr.
2 When does Id-ul-Fitr start?
3 What is Zakat-ul-Fitr used for?

TASK BOX

a) Explain why Id-ul-Fitr is sometimes called the Day of Reward.
b) Explain why Muslims attend mosque at Id-ul-Fitr.
c) Explain why Muslims remember the poor at Id-ul-Fitr.

◄ A family in their festival clothes give money at the mosque.

▲ A zakah box.

> Righteous is he who believeth in Allah ... and giveth his wealth, for love of Him, to kinsfolk and to orphans and the needy and the wayfarer and to those who ask, and to set slaves free; and observeth proper worship and payeth the poor-due.
>
> *Qur'an 2:177 (Pickthall)*

> Lo! Those who believe and do good works and establish worship and pay the poor-due, their reward is with their Lord and there shall no fear come upon them neither shall they grieve.
>
> *Qur'an 2:277 (Pickthall)*

Many Muslims pay **zakah** at this time (as well as Zakat-ul-Fitr). Zakah is an obligatory poor-tax, or poor-due. It is so important that it is set beside worship in the former quotations. Indeed, it is regarded as an act of worship itself, since it is the Third Pillar of Islam.

Zakah is a type of charity to help the needy in Islam; but Muslims prefer to use the words 'poor-due', since people have a duty to pay it and the poor have a right to receive it (and should not refuse it when it is offered). It is given to those in need, such as poor families, students, and even Islamic organisations in need of financial assistance. It is a relatively small tax of about 2.5 per cent of a person's wealth. (There

are complicated rules for working it out.) Those who have no surplus wealth are not required to pay zakah, but will be the recipients of it.

In some Islamic countries, zakah is collected by the government; in others it is regarded as a private matter. Muslims in the West often send money to those in Third World countries, like Bangladesh, showing the sense of brotherhood between Muslims throughout the world.

Zakah is Islam's way of redistributing wealth, to make a fairer society. Islam teaches that all our blessings come from Allah, and we should show our gratitude both by enjoying them ourselves, and also by sharing them with others. The word *zakah* means 'purification'. Muslims believe that giving some of their wealth helps to purify them of greed and selfishness. Zakah also aims to purify society of the evil divisions between rich and poor. Many Muslims will want to give away more than the required amount, and their religion encourages them to do so. Voluntary charity is called **sadaqah**.

TEST YOURSELF

1 What is zakah?
2 What does the word 'zakah' mean?
3 What percentage of a Muslim's money should be given annually for zakah?

WHAT DOES ISLAM TEACH ABOUT WEALTH?

>
> Spend your wealth for the cause of Allah, and be not cast by your own hands to ruin; and do good. Lo! Allah loveth the beneficent.
>
> *Qur'an 2:195 (Pickthall)*

Zakah is about giving away money. It is a way of distributing wealth in a community, so that the needy are cared for. Islam encourages people to be charitable, but to do this out of concern for the needy and not to show off. The Qur'an says that if someone owes you money and cannot pay it back, you should give him time to pay or, better still, let him keep it. Muslims are forbidden to lend someone money and charge interest on the loan, because this makes it more difficult for poor people to get out of debt.

Islam has clear rules about how people should gain money. It can be inherited, but there are rules to make sure that this is distributed fairly. Most money should be earned by honest work. Islam teaches that money should not simply make more money, for example, through investment (otherwise the rich will simply get richer). Charging interest on loans of money (called **riba**) is forbidden. This has made it difficult for Muslims to use Western banks, because they charge interest on loans and give interest on savings. It is particularly difficult for them to buy property in Western countries, because mortgages are basically loans on which the bank charges interest. Some Muslims have dealt with this by putting their money together to buy a property; but sometimes property prices go up much faster than people can save. In 2003 the HSBC Bank established 'Amanah Finance' for Muslims, in accordance with Islamic law (Shariah). It makes it possible for Muslims to buy property, not through a normal mortgage, but by renting the property from the bank and making a monthly contribution towards the purchase price until they have paid for it. So the bank originally buys the property and owns it on behalf of a Muslim client until he or she has fully paid for it.

There are ways in which Muslim banks can use money, but it must support ethical business and not activities such as gambling or the sale of alcohol. In supporting these ventures, Muslims must be prepared to take losses as well as gains, rather than being guaranteed a set rate of interest. And, once a year, Muslims pay zakah on all their wealth, not just their earnings.

HSBC Amanah Finance

financing in accordance with Shariah

HSBC ‹X›
The world's local bank

▲ HSBC Bank has special arrangements for its Muslim customers.

TASK BOX

Discuss the following:
a) Do you think we should give money to charity? Try to think of arguments both for and against before coming to your own conclusion.
b) 'What I do with my money is my affair.' Give an Islamic response to this statement.

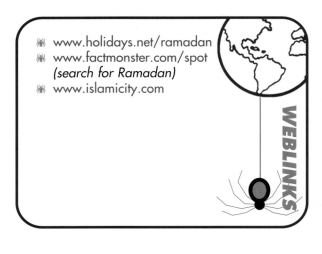

www.holidays.net/ramadan

www.factmonster.com/spot
(search for Ramadan)

www.islamicity.com

WEBLINKS

1 a) Describe how the month of Ramadan is different from other months for practising Muslims.

b) Explain the reasons why Muslims must fast.

c) 'Fasting is a waste of effort.'
Do you agree?
Give reasons for your answer, showing that you have thought about different points of view. You must refer to Islam in your answer.

Assignment

6

UNIT SIX | Pilgrimage

KEY WORDS

Dhul–Hijjah: month of pilgrimage.
Hajj: the Greater Pilgrimage, the Fifth Pillar of Islam.
hajja: woman who has completed the Hajj.
hajji: man who has completed the Hajj.
haram: forbidden/sacred.
Id–ul–Adha: the festival at the end of the Hajj.
ihram: pilgrim clothes; state of consecration.
Ka'bah: the building in the centre of the Sacred Mosque in Makkah.
kiswah: the cloth that covers the Ka'bah.
Makkah: holiest city of Islam.
pilgrimage: a journey to a holy place, for religious purposes.
Sa'y: ritual 'Running' between Mounts As-Safa and Al-Marwa.
Tawaf: ritual 'Circling' of the Ka'bah.
Umrah: the Lesser Pilgrimage.
Ummah: the worldwide Muslim community.

KEY QUESTION

What does the Hajj entail and why do Muslims do it?

WHY DO MUSLIMS WISH TO VISIT MAKKAH?

A pilgrim is someone who travels to a holy place, for religious devotions. The most important place of **pilgrimage** for Muslims is, of course, Makkah. Not only was Muhammad born in Makkah and lived there most of his life, but he himself performed religious rituals there.

Makkah had been a holy city long before Muhammad reclaimed it for Allah. He encouraged the continuation of many of the old practices, but purified them by restoring what he believed to be their true meaning, in the worship of the One God.

So pilgrims to Makkah are walking in the footsteps of Muhammad, performing the same rituals that he did on pilgrimage all those years ago. Even more important than following the Prophet's example, is the fact that pilgrimage is commanded in the Qur'an.

Perform the pilgrimage and the visit (to Mecca) for Allah.

Qur'an 2:196 (Pickthall)

It is the duty of all men towards God to come to the House a pilgrim, if he is able to make his way there.

Qur'an 3:93 (Arberry)

And proclaim among men the Pilgrimage, and they shall come unto thee on foot and upon every lean beast, they shall come from every deep ravine.

Qur'an 22:27 (Arberry)

▲ In the Sacred Mosque in Makkah. Each year, two million Muslims from all over the world come together for Hajj.

▲ On returning from Hajj, Muslims often decorate the walls of their houses with appropriate symbols.

A New Approach – Islam

The Fifth Pillar of Islam makes it an obligation (**fard**) for all Muslims to perform the Greater Pilgrimage at least once in their lives, if possible. To fail to do so, when they are able, is regarded as a grave sin. Yet only about one in ten Muslims manages to do it, because they have to fulfil the following requirements.

- They must have reached the age of responsibility and be of sound mind, so that they know what they are doing. Although children are sometimes taken with their parents on pilgrimage, this does not count for them as fulfilling the Fifth Pillar.
- They must be able to afford it. Therefore, they should have no debts; and they should have gained the money to pay for the pilgrimage through honest means.
- They should be physically fit. It is advisable for Muslims to go on pilgrimage when they are young enough to withstand the gruelling conditions. Unfortunately, many cannot afford it until their old age, and some die on the pilgrimage.

The Greater Pilgrimage is called the **Hajj**; those who manage to complete it are honoured with the titles of **hajji** (for a man) and **hajja** (for a woman). The word hajj literally means 'to set out for a definite purpose'. As you read the rest of this unit, think about its meaning and importance for Muslims – its religious purpose.

WHAT DOES THE GREATER PILGRIMAGE CONSIST OF?

The Greater Pilgrimage is called the Hajj, and this can only be done on special days during the pilgrimage month – **Dhul-Hijjah**. This is what it involves (all of which will be explained in detail later in the unit):

- Wearing the **ihram**.
- Travelling towards Arafat on 8 Dhul-Hijjah (and staying at Mina overnight).
- 'Standing' at Arafat from noon to dusk on 9 Dhul-Hijja.
- 'Stoning the Devil' and making an animal sacrifice at Mina on 10 Dhul-Hija.

- Cutting or shaving the hair.
- Making the **Tawaf**, the 'Circling' of the Ka'bah in Makkah.
- Further 'Stoning of the Devil' at Mina on 11, 12 (and 13) Dhul-Hijja.

When a pilgrim finally leaves Makkah, he or she will perform a Farewell Circling of the Ka'bah.

The Hajj itself takes only five or six days, but pilgrims will need time to perform the Umrah, the Lesser Pilgrimage, as well (notice that this means doing some rituals twice), and will therefore arrive in Makkah some days before 8 Dhul-Hijjah. Many, coming from afar on this journey of a lifetime, like to extend the trip to have more time at Makkah and Mina, and to go on to visit Madinah, the second holy city in Islam. In 2004, a Hajj travel agent in London charged pilgrims £2600 for a complete two-week package, or £2950 for a three-week package.

WHAT IS THE LESSER PILGRIMAGE?

On visiting Makkah, at any time of the year, Muslims are required to perform the **Umrah**, the Lesser Pilgrimage. This is what it involves:

- Wearing the ihram, the pilgrim's clothes, before approaching Makkah.
- Making the Tawaf, the ritual 'Circling' of the Ka'bah seven times.
- Making the **Sa'y**, the ritual 'Running' between Mounts As-Safa and Al-Marwa seven times.

> ### TEST YOURSELF
> **A B C**
> 1. What is a pilgrimage?
> 2. Which pilgrimage is the fifth of the Five Pillars?
> 3. In which month does this take place?
> 4. What is the Lesser Pilgrimage?
> 5. Where is Makkah?

Why can only Muslims visit Makkah?

The Qur'an calls Makkah 'the mother town' (42:7) because it is the spiritual centre of Islam. Each year at Hajj, pilgrims arrive there in their hundreds of thousands, by road, sea and air. As they approach Makkah, there are signs warning that only Muslims are allowed into the holy city. The area of the Hajj is **haram**. This word means both 'forbidden' and 'sacred', i.e. it is so special that it is set apart for a holy purpose, and those who are not Muslims are therefore forbidden. The mosque in which the Ka'bah stands is called the **Masjid al-Haram**, the Sacred Mosque. The boundary lies between about 5 and 30 kilometres from the Ka'bah; and everyone is stopped on the approaches to the city to have their passes checked.

What do Muslims wear for the Hajj?

Before reaching the sacred city, pilgrims must purify their bodies (preferably with a full bath, or else by performing wudu, see p.18), and enter into a state of holiness called **ihram**. This word literally means 'consecration', or dedication to holy things. The special dress worn by pilgrims is also called ihram. For men, it consists of two pieces of unsewn white cloth: one tied round the waist, the other thrown over the left shoulder. They have nothing on their heads (which is why many carry umbrellas, for protection against the sun), and are only permitted to have sandals on their feet. There is no such uniform for women, but they must be fully covered, apart from the hands and face. Many wear simple long white dresses with head-scarves.

▲ Pilgrims in ihram dress reach Jeddah airport in Saudi Arabia.

A New Approach – Islam

Ihram is an important symbol for Muslims. It has the following meanings:

- They have entered a state of holiness. It is a reminder that they are performing special, sacred rituals.
- They have put off all that connects them with their usual lives, in order to concentrate totally on Allah.
- Dressed so simply, it is a sign of humility before Allah.
  (The ihram clothes are similar to those in which a new-born child is wrapped. They can therefore remind a Muslim of the day he first came into the world as a helpless baby. Also, the ihram wraps will be kept for the pilgrim's burial. So wearing them now reminds the pilgrim that he comes before Allah, stripped of all material goods and status, just as he will be at death.)
- White is a symbol of purity. It is a reminder that they must try not to sin.
- Muslims are all dressed the same because they are equal in the sight of Allah.

Once in the state of ihram, pilgrims must not worry over their personal appearance, so they cannot wear perfume or jewellery. They must be particularly mindful of Allah's laws, and must therefore avoid all violence, even to animals, plants and insects. They must treat the pilgrimage as a sacrifice to Allah, and must abstain from sexual relationships during that time. (Many husbands and wives travel together, but stay in separate accommodation.) In short, they must devote themselves wholly to Allah for this brief but intense period of their lives. This is

▲ Pilgrims have to change into 'ihram' – their pilgrim clothes – before entering Makkah (where they can be distinguished from the ordinary residents).

expressed in the frequent pilgrim calls in Arabic which mean 'Doubly at your service, O God'.

Makkah is now part of modern Saudi Arabia, and the king is the guardian of the Muslim shrines there. Each year the Saudi government goes to great trouble to organise and accommodate all the pilgrims. In Makkah, they are divided into groups with an official guide to look after them and instruct them in the rituals.

TASK BOX

a) Explain why Makkah is the most important city in Islam and Madinah is the second in importance.

b) Explain the significance of the ihram clothes worn by pilgrims on the Hajj.

c) Explain why most Muslims do not manage to do the Hajj, even though it is one of the Pillars of Islam.

Discuss the following:

Do you think Islam is right to ban non-Muslims from its holiest sites? Give arguments for and against before coming to your own opinion.

WHY IS THE KA'BAH SO IMPORTANT?

The first thing that any Muslim pilgrim will want to see is the building towards which he or she turns in prayer five times a day: the holy **Ka'bah**. Set in the courtyard of the Sacred Mosque in Makkah, it is 15.25 metres high, made of large stone blocks, and cube-shaped (*ka'bah* means 'cube'). It is covered with a beautiful black silk cloth, called the **Kiswah**. This is made in Makkah and has words of the Qur'an embroidered on it in gold thread. The edges of the Kiswah are hoisted up during the Hajj; and towards the end of Hajj, on 10 Dhul-Hijjah, it is replaced each year with a new one. The old cloth is cut up and sent to various Muslim organisations throughout the world. It is regarded as a great honour to be able to frame a piece and hang it on the wall.

For a Muslim, the Ka'bah has layer upon layer of tradition and meaning attached to it. It is said to be the first house of prayer on earth. Legend has it that Adam was sent down from heaven and wandered the earth until he reached Arabia. There he wanted to build a house of prayer like the one in heaven. One story says that Allah let down a replica out of heaven; others that Adam built it himself.

Later, Ibrahim is said to have rebuilt the Ka'bah, with the help of his son Isma'il. The Station of Ibrahim now stands in the courtyard of the Sacred Mosque in Makkah, marking the spot from which it is believed he began the building operations. Tradition tells that Ibrahim also prayed at this spot, and pilgrims are required to do the same.

> And when We made the house (at Mecca) a resort for mankind and a sanctuary, (saying): Take as your place of worship the place where Abraham stood (to pray). And We imposed a duty upon Abraham and Ishmael, (saying): Purify My house for those who go around and those who meditate therein and those who bow down and prostrate themselves (in worship).
>
> *Qur'an 2:125 (Pickthall)*

▲ The Station of Ibrahim. It contains a boulder on which he is said to have stood when directing the building operations for the Ka'bah.

▲ The Ka'bah

Ibrahim's Egyptian wife was called Hajar, who bore him Isma'il, his eldest son. There is an open area in front of the Ka'bah, enclosed by a semi-circular wall, marking the traditional site of the graves of Hajar and Isma'il. Low down, set into the wall in one corner of the Ka'bah, is the Black Stone. It is a very ancient stone, probably a meteorite (it is believed to have come down from heaven). One tradition is that it was originally white, but turned black as a result of people's sin.

There is a story about the Black Stone and Muhammad when he was a young man in Makkah. The Ka'bah was being repaired and the Black Stone had been removed. When the time came to replace it, the four leading families in Makkah argued over who should have the privilege.

They finally agreed that it should be decided by the next person to enter the Sacred Mosque – and that was Muhammad. With great diplomacy, Muhammad refused to choose a representative from any one family. Instead, he told each to take hold of a corner of a cloak in which the stone would be carried to the Ka'bah. Then Muhammad himself lifted out the stone and restored it to its place.

The Black Stone is now set in the wall in a silver surround, like a big inverted bowl with an opening in the centre. The stone has a deep hollow in its middle, where it has been worn away by the kisses of millions of pilgrims through the ages (see p.27). Muhammad himself encouraged this practice. Those pilgrims who cannot get close enough to kiss or touch it in the crowds, raise their hand to it as they pass.

There is a door into the Ka'bah, but it is rarely used, because the building has been empty since Muhammad destroyed the idols that it housed, back in 630CE. Muhammad restored the Ka'bah to what he believed had been its original purpose – the centre for the worship of the One God.

▲ This used to be fixed to the corner of the Ka'bah, surrounding the Black Stone.

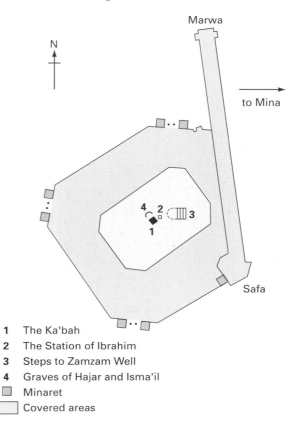

1 The Ka'bah
2 The Station of Ibrahim
3 Steps to Zamzam Well
4 Graves of Hajar and Isma'il
▢ Minaret
▢ Covered areas

A plan of the Sacred Mosque. ▶

WHAT IS TAWAF – THE CIRCLING?

Pilgrims move around the Ka'bah in an anti-clockwise direction, seven times (preferably running the first three, and walking the last four). They start and finish counting the circuits from the corner where the Black Stone is. If at all possible, they should kiss or touch this stone, since Muhammad used to do this, or at least salute it as they go by.

The Circling demonstrates the unity of the believers in the worship of the One God, as they move in harmony together around their central shrine, each reciting an individual verse of the Qur'an. At the end of the Circling, they go to the Station of Ibrahim to pray two rak'ahs.

▼ Pilgrims circle the Ka'bah together seven times.

WHAT IS SA'Y – THE RUNNING?

There is a covered way which extends out from the Sacred Mosque, and is built between two hills, called As-Safa and Al-Marwa. Pilgrims must hurry along this passage, seven times, beginning at As-Safa which is nearest to the Sacred Mosque, and finishing at Al-Marwa. There is a corridor down the middle for those who are being pushed in wheelchairs; the other pilgrims pass on either side, in one direction only.

In performing this ritual, pilgrims are re-enacting Hajar's frantic search for water when left in the desert with her young son Isma'il. The story tells how they were saved from dying of thirst. Isma'il dug his heels into the sand, where Hajar had left him, and a spring of water gushed up.

Pilgrims can still visit this spring, at the Zamzam Well. There are steps leading down to it, in a chamber under the courtyard of the Sacred Mosque. Many pilgrims bathe the edge of their ihram in it, and take some of the water home with them.

▲ A special, covered walkway enables pilgrims to move back and forth between Mounts Safa and Marwa.

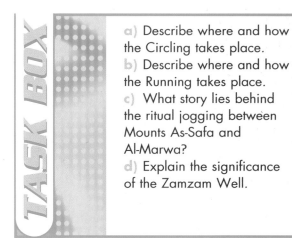

WHY IS THE DAY OF ARAFAT SO IMPORTANT?

The Plain of Arafat lies about 24 kilometres east of Makkah, in hilly terrain, with the Mount of Mercy in the centre. Pilgrims must be there for the period from noon to dusk on 9 Dhul-Hijja. Some gather there the previous evening, but most come on from Mina (about 10 kilometres from Makkah) after the dawn prayer.

The most important part of the Hajj is the 'Standing before Allah' at Arafat, where pilgrims beg forgiveness of their sins. It is an amazing sight to see about 2 million people out in the relentless heat of the desert and swarming over the Mount of Mercy, engrossed in their devotions. It calls to mind for Muslims the Day of Judgement, as the following passage shows. It is from an article entitled 'Journey to Mercy'.

Pilgrims perform the noon and afternoon prayers together at Arafat, then move off at dusk to spend the night at Muzdalifah, where they perform the sunset and night prayers.

PERSPECTIVES

Witnessing this, one cannot but think of the Day of Reckoning which we must all keep in mind every minute of every day. The day of Arafat is extremely difficult. How much more difficult will that day be. On the day of Arafat you beg God's mercy. On the day of Reckoning you need God's mercy. It is for that day that you must seriously consider fulfilling every pillar of the pledge as a Muslim. It is for that that you should plan to complete Hajj as soon as you are capable, for Hajj is one way you may, if Allah wills, erase all your sins, secure for yourself forgiveness and ensure Allah's mercy.

From Islamic Cultural Centre Newsletter No.31, for Dhul-Hijja

▲ Pilgrims 'standing before Allah' on the Mount of Mercy.

A New Approach – Islam

WHAT IS IT LIKE AT MINA?

However well organised it is, there are bound to be safety risks when so many people gather together for this sort of religious occasion. Most years there are reports of accidents and deaths, but the following news cuttings (below and on the next page) report a particularly bad fire that swept through the tent city on the plain of Mina in 1997. They indicate some of the problems facing the Saudi Arabian government in its guardianship of the pilgrim sites.

---

300 feared dead as fire sweeps Mecca tent city

Disaster struck the annual pilgrimage to Mecca yesterday, when as many as 300 people died in a terrifying fire. In 1994, hundreds of Indonesian pilgrims were killed when they surged forward in the ceremony of 'stoning the devil' which is part of the Hajj ritual. In 1990, 1,426 people were crushed to death in a tunnel leading to holy sites and in 1987, 402 Iranians were killed in a fight with Saudi security forces.

Over the past ten years Saudi Arabia has spent $18.6bn (£11.4bn) providing facilities for the pilgrims. Some 150,000 security forces, guides and boy scouts have been mobilised by the kingdom to oversee the Hajj, the largest gathering of people in the world.

About half of the 2 million pilgrims are foreign – some 60,000 of them Iranian – and the rest Saudi Arabian. Saudi Arabian Airlines has transported an estimated 600,000 pilgrims from 60 destinations around the world.

The Independent,
16 April 1997

▲ An aerial view over the tent city at Mina.

Saudis clear debris of Mecca's hellish pilgrimage inferno

The Saudi Arabian authorities in Mecca were yesterday trying to identify the bodies of 343 Muslim pilgrims who burned to death in the fire which engulfed their tent city as they attended the Hajj pilgrimage. A further 1,290 people are known to have suffered injuries as the flames, fanned by the wind, spread rapidly through the 70,000 tents pitched on the plain of Mina outside the holy city of Mecca.

In the remains of the Mina encampment, trucks were beginning yesterday to cart away burned wreckage of everything from charred water bottles to refrigerators, air conditioners and buses, which caught fire as strong winds spread the flames. The cause of the blaze is being attributed to an exploding gas cylinder, often used for cooking food and making coffee and tea by many of the two million Hajj pilgrims.

The Independent,
17 April 1997

WHAT IS THE STONING OF THE DEVIL?

The next day, on 10 Dhul-Hijja, the pilgrims arrive at Mina, where the 'Stoning of the Devil' takes place. On this day, they throw seven small pebbles at the pillar known as the 'Great Devil'. The ritual continues on 11 and 12 Dhul-Hijjah, when they throw seven pebbles at each of three pillars (hence 49 pebbles in all). Some pilgrims continue the practice into 13 Dhul-Hijja (hence 70 pebbles in all).

The police are well in attendance at the pillars, since this ritual can be dangerous, if the pilgrims get carried away with it. A Hajj handbook gives the warning: 'What is prescribed is to be gentle and to throw the pebbles without hurting anyone.' (*A Guide to Hajj*, Umrah and Visitat to the Prophet's Mosque, pp.50–51.) However, there is a history of stampedes and fatalities as those at the back surge forward, crushing pilgrims nearest to the pillars.

▲ 'Stoning the Devil' at Mina.

▲ 'King Faud of Saudi Arabia has ordered a comprehensive plan to be drawn up to improve the safety of pilgrims in the holy cities of Mecca and Medina. The royal decree was issued within hours of last Sunday's stampede ... in which an estimated 250 pilgrims died.' *Church Times, 6.2.04*, Gerald Butt, Middle East Correspondent

What is the purpose of this ritual?

There are two reasons behind it. Firstly, it reminds pilgrims of the famous story of Ibrahim and his son Isma'il, in which Allah tested their faith by asking Ibrahim to sacrifice his son to him. Three times the devil tempted Ibrahim not to do it, and tempted Isma'il to run away. But both father and son withstood the temptations, and they drove away the devil by throwing stones at him. They were prepared to go through with the sacrifice, in obedience to Allah's command, and out of love for Allah. Then, at the last moment, Allah stopped Ibrahim's hand, and provided a ram for sacrifice instead.

The other purpose and meaning of this ritual is a much more personal one. As the pilgrims 'Stone the Devil', they are expressing their own rejection of evil and their own resolve to withstand any temptations which may come their way.

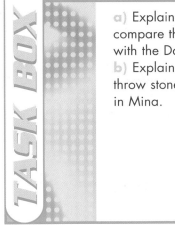

TASK BOX

a) Explain why Muslims compare the Day of Arafat with the Day of Judgement.
b) Explain why pilgrims throw stones at the pillars in Mina.

WHY DO PILGRIMS OFFER A SACRIFICE?

Pilgrims on Hajj are obliged, if they can afford it, to offer an animal for sacrifice. This is done at Mina, where the meat is roasted and enjoyed by the pilgrims, but at least a third of it must be given to those who are too poor to buy their own animal. (Since there is too much meat to distribute all at once, the Saudi government has now installed refrigeration for it, at Mina.)

This sacrifice is another reminder of the story of Ibrahim and Isma'il, since a ram was given to Ibrahim to sacrifice instead of his son. By sacrificing animals, Muslims recognise that the meat we eat is a gift from Allah which should never be taken for granted. Also, since animals are very expensive, it is a sign that Muslims are prepared to give up things for their religion.

After making this sacrifice, pilgrims can change out of their ihram and rest for a while before putting on the ihram again and completing the rituals of the Hajj. It is at this stage in the proceedings that they have their hair cut (a woman may just have a lock of hair snipped off; a man may have his whole head shaved). This is a sign that they are coming out of the state of consecration.

HOW IS ID-UL-ADHA CELEBRATED?

Id-ul-Adha means the 'Major Festival', and it is also called the 'Festival of Sacrifice'. For while the pilgrims are sacrificing their animals near to the holy city of Makkah, Muslims all over the world are joining them in making an animal sacrifice: a goat or sheep per family, or a cow or camel between a larger group.

In Muslim countries, animals are usually bought a few weeks before Id and sacrificed on Id day in the backyard. In Britain, a special licence is needed to slaughter animals. So Muslims go along to their local slaughterhouse, where the animal's throat is slit in the traditional way, with the Bismillah said over it. There is a lot of controversy in Western countries over the ritual slaughter of animals. Scientists cannot agree which method causes least pain and trauma; but Muslims believe that their method is the kindest, quickest and least painful form of death.

A third of the meat is eaten by the family which bought it; a third is given to friends and relatives; and a third given to the poor. In Western countries it may be given to an old people's home. Some Muslims in the West send money to Pakistan or India, to pay for an animal to be sacrificed there instead and given to the poor.

▲ A kiosk where pilgrims on the Hajj can pay for their sacrificial animal.

▲ A Muslim in Jerusalem, Israel, buys a sheep for Id-ul-Adha.

A New Approach – Islam

The meaning of this sacrifice is the same as for those on the Hajj.

- It reminds Muslims of the story of Ibrahim and Isma'il, and of their willingness to make great sacrifices for Allah.
- It shows their own readiness to make sacrifices for their religion.
- It is a way of giving thanks to the Creator God for the meat they eat.
- It shows their concern to share their wealth with the poor.

In addition:

- It is a way for the Muslims back home to show their support for their fellow Muslims who are completing the Hajj.

Like Id-ul-Fitr, this festival is a holiday from school or work (lasting three days in Muslim countries), and begins with congregational prayers in the mosque. People dress up in their best clothes, send each other cards and gifts, and share meals with each other.

TASK BOX

Discuss the following:

a) Do you think the Islamic way of killing animals is any better or worse than methods allowed in Britain?
b) Do you think sacrificing animals gives meat-eaters more respect for animal life?

▲ Pilgrims gathered in Makkah illustrate Ummah – the worldwide fellowship of Muslims (see overpage).

What is the Ummah?

The photograph of pilgrims on the previous page is a perfect expression of the **Ummah**, the Islamic community. It is the worldwide fellowship of Muslims which transcends race, nationality, colour, gender and language. There are many indications of this brotherhood within Islam, but nowhere is it more obvious than on the Hajj.

The Hajj gathers together about two million people each year, for a common purpose – the largest annual gathering of people anywhere in the world, as the extract opposite from a Muslim newsletter states:

The Hajj is a unique annual conference, convened by Allah Subhanahu wa Ta'ala. He has ordained its time, prescribed its place, selected the participants and ordered its programme . . . Hajj should make Muslims the envy of the world, for no other nation on earth can boast or co-ordinate a conference of such magnitude every year, bringing Muslims together from all over the globe . . . to meet in unity of mind and spirit, brotherhood and understanding.

(Subhanahu wa Ta'ala means Glorified and Exalted.)

Editorial ICC Newsletter, No.31

There are many other examples of Islamic fellowship.

- Muslims all over the world face the Ka'bah when they pray. It is therefore a sign of unity, as the focus of their prayers. This point is made even more strongly when you see crowds of Muslims praying in the courtyard all round the Ka'bah, or performing the ritual Circling of the Ka'bah together.
- Whenever Muslims pray together, they stand in lines, shoulder to shoulder, to emphasise their unity with each other. And at the end of the prayers, they turn to bless their fellow Muslims on their right and on their left. At Hajj, you can see two million pilgrims doing this at Arafat, when they perform the noon and afternoon prayers, standing in orderly rows and going through the prayer motions together.
- When pilgrims put on their ihram, they are all dressed alike. There is no distinction between rich or poor, king or commoner. Again, this is a sign of unity.
- When pilgrims are making the sacrifice at Mina, Muslims throughout the world are joining in the animal sacrifice.
- Their concern for their Muslim brothers and sisters who are poor is shown in the sharing of the sacrificial meat on the Hajj.
- Whether or not they come from Arabic-speaking countries, all Muslims learn the Arabic Qur'an and the Arabic words for salah. So, although the many pilgrims speak in a multitude of different languages, they can all join together in the same language for worship.
- The Islamic Empire, once known as **Dar-ul-Islam**, the 'House of Islam', no longer exists; but there is still a sense of responsibility between one Islamic state and another. It can be seen at the Hajj, when the Saudi royal house, as guardian of the sacred cities of Makkah and Madinah, takes a paternal role towards the pilgrims who come there from all over the world. Saudi Arabia's oil wealth has also enabled it to give aid to some of the poor Islamic countries, like Pakistan.

The importance of the Ummah is summed up in this final quotation:

Those who believe obtain their strength by believing that they are but one brotherhood. Allah Subhanahu wa Ta'ala says in the Holy Qur'an: 'Those who believe are but one single brotherhood.' Therefore true believers feel for their brothers and sisters and they likewise for them. They should help each other wherever they are, look after each other when unwell, guard their belongings while they are away, support them in their needs especially when their lives are in danger, keep them company when they are alone, support them in their struggle for earning their livelihood. By doing so, then each individual's strength becomes the strength of all the believers'.

'Friday Khutba', ICC Newsletter No.43

 Consider what these ahadith mean:

Each of you is a mirror of his brother, if you see something wrong in your brother, you must tell him to get rid of it.

Tirmidhi

Believers are like the parts of a building to one another – each part supporting the others.

Bukhari

None of you can be a believer unless he loves for his brother what he loves for himself.

Bukhari

A Muslim is he from whose tongue and hands other Muslims are safe.

Bukhari

REMEMBER

▶ **Muslims should try to perform the Hajj at least once in their lifetime. It is the Fifth Pillar of Islam.**
▶ **The Hajj takes place in and around Makkah, following in the footsteps of Muhammad.**
▶ **During the Hajj, pilgrims are in a holy state, which is shown by the special clothes they wear.**
▶ **The most important part of the Hajj is the Day of Arafat, when pilgrims climb the Mount of Mercy to ask for Allah's forgiveness of their sins.**
▶ **The Hajj finishes with the festival of Id-ul-Adha, which is celebrated by Muslims all over the world.**

WEBLINKS

- www.channel4.com/life/microsites/H/hajj *(to go through the Hajj day by day)*
- www.ummah.org.uk/hajj/
- www.the-webplaza.com/hajj/index.shtml
- www.mcb.org.uk/hajjadvice.html *(advice to pilgrims from The Muslim Council of Britain)*
- www.haj.co.uk *(for a Hajj and Umra travel company in the UK)*

---

1 a) Describe the Sacred Mosque at Makkah and the rituals that pilgrims perform there.

b) Explain why the Ka'bah is so important to Muslims.

c) 'It isn't necessary to go on pilgrimage to feel close to God.' How far do you agree with this statement? Give reasons to support your answer and show that you have thought about different points of view, including those of Islam.

Assignment

UNIT SEVEN | The Growth of Islam

7

KEY WORDS

'Ashura: day of remembrance for the death of Husayn at Karbala.
Caliph: successor to Muhammad.
Companions: Muslims who knew Muhammad.
dhikr: remembrance of Allah's names, a practice often done with prayer beads.
Imams: Shi'ite leaders.
Mahdi: the one expected before the Day of Judgement.
shaikh/sheikh: leader of a Sufi Order.
Shari'ah: Islamic law.
Shi'ahs, Shi'is or Shi'ites: followers of the Shi'ah, Shi'ism or Shi'i Islam.
Sufism: branch of Islam that emphasises personal religious experiences.
Sunnah: Islamic way of life established by Muhammad.
Sunni: main branch of Islam.
tariqah: the Sufi way or path.

KEY QUESTION

Where did Islam spread after the death of Muhammad?

SPREAD OF THE ISLAMIC EMPIRES

622–34

Muhammad had managed to unite most of Arabia under Islam. This was a remarkable achievement, considering that many of the Arabian tribes had been feuding with each other for centuries. On his death, many of these tribes broke away again. During Abu Bakr's brief caliphate of two years, he was able to suppress this revolt.

634–44

Umar, the second **Caliph**, took Islam beyond Arabia. First, his armies invaded Palestine, with its holy city of Jerusalem; and then they went beyond into Syria where they took the capital city, Damascus, in 635. In 642, Alexandria in Egypt was captured, and the march continued along the coast of North Africa into Libya. The following year, in the east of his empire, Isfahan in Persia (Iran) was taken.

644–56

Uthman, the third Caliph, continued to push out the frontiers of the Islamic empire on all sides, reaching the borders of Afghanistan in the east.

656–661

Ali, the fourth Caliph, moved his capital to Kufa in Iraq and tried to consolidate the empire.

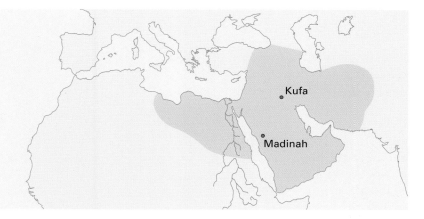

661–750

The Islamic empire continued to expand under the Umayyad Dynasty, which ruled from Damascus in Syria (and not Madinah). It reached the borders of India in the East. In 732, exactly a century after Muhammad's death, it reached its furthest point west, in France, where the Muslims were turned back at Tours by Charles Martel.

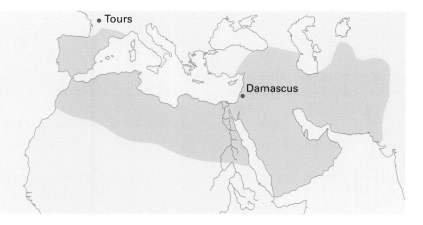

The 'Abbasid Caliphate

Some of the Umayyad caliphs were irreligious and corrupt, and they were finally overthrown (except in Spain) by the 'Abbasids who were descended from Muhammad's uncle al-'Abbas. They ruled from their new capital of Baghdad in Iraq. The 'Abbasid Dynasty was powerful for about 150 years, after which the Islamic empire was split up under a number of different dynasties.

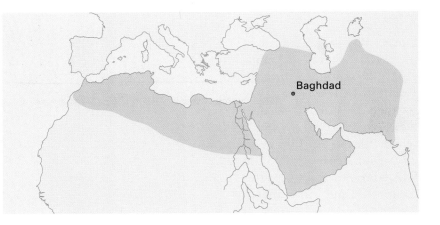

The Ottoman Caliphate

It was only with the rise of the Ottoman empire that most of the Islamic lands (except Iran, India and Central Asia) were united again. The great Ottoman empire lasted longer than any of the others, from the early sixteenth century into the twentieth century. It was ruled from Istanbul in Turkey. However, the First World War saw the break-up of the Islamic empire, and the caliphate was ended in 1924.

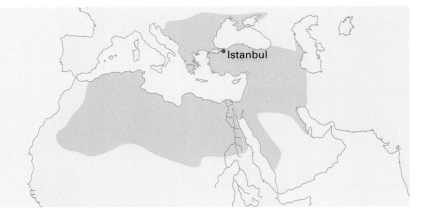

TEST YOURSELF

A B C Name the capital cities connected with the following:
1 Muhammad
2 the early Caliphs
3 the Umayyad Dynasty
4 the 'Abbasid Dynasty
5 the Ottoman empire

▲ Part of the Alhambra Palace, Granada, Spain. The Muslims ruled this country for seven centuries. Wherever Islam has spread, it has left a legacy of beautiful Muslim architecture, with its intricate patterns, calligraphy, and delicately moulded stucco work.

KEY QUESTION

Why were the first four caliphs called the 'Rightly Guided'?

WHO WERE THE FIRST FOUR CALIPHS?

Who was Abu Bakr, the first Caliph (632–34CE)?

Muhammad had not stated clearly who should succeed him and so become caliph ('successor') and ruler of the Islamic empire. In the uncertainty following his death, Abu Bakr was hastily chosen and accepted by the majority.

There was much to commend him. He was one of Muhammad's closest friends, a

Companion (see p.31) from the very early days of Islam in Makkah. Muhammad had honoured him by marrying his daughter Ayesha. Abu Bakr belonged to the leading Quraish tribe, as had Muhammad, and was therefore more likely to be accepted by the various Arab tribesmen. He had a reputation as a good and holy man, and he continued to live humbly and in simplicity to the end of his life, caring for orphans and slaves. He defended Makkah against attacks and collected together the material to form the Qur'an.

Who was Umar, the second Caliph (634–44CE)?

Before Abu Bakr died in 634, he named Umar as his successor. Umar too was an early Companion of Muhammad, but in character he was very different from Abu Bakr. Umar was a big, strong man who had to learn to control a violent temper. There is a famous story of his conversion to Islam. He went to his sister's house to try to stop her from being a Muslim, and he even struck her, but when he read the words she had from the Qur'an he was completely won over by them. From that time onwards he became a faithful friend and supporter of the Prophet.

This account of how Umar and Abu Bakr reacted to Muhammad's death also shows up the difference between the two men:

> We all know what happened when the Prophet (Peace be upon him) died. At the time the Muslims found it very difficult to accept his death, they felt insecure and confused. Umar's immediate reaction was to angrily proclaim – 'If anyone dares to say that the Prophet (Peace be upon him) is dead, I will kill him with this sword.' Alhamdullilah, on the contrary, Abu Bakr's reaction was clear and lucid, as he said: 'If there is anyone amongst you who worshipped Muhammad, Muhammad is dead, but, whoever worshipped Allah Subhana Wa Ta'ala, Allah is always there. He is eternal.' (May Allah be pleased with them both.)

'Friday Khutba', ICC Newsletter No.43

(Alhamdullilah means 'all praise is due to Allah'; Allah Subhana Wa Ta'ala means 'Allah be glorified and exalted'.)

▲ Muslims in Cairo, Egypt (where Islam spread during Umar's caliphate).

Umar was a great soldier, and during his reign he extended the Islamic empire beyond Arabia into Syria, Iraq and Egypt. But, for all his military power, he was a saintly man. Like Abu Bakr and Muhammad himself, he lived in simplicity, caring little for his own comfort. He was known for his good treatment of those he conquered, particularly the Jews and Christians, the 'People of the Book'. He introduced a tax system to aid the poor and elderly and also to pay the soldiers so that they did not need to loot captured towns and villages.

Who was Uthman, the third Caliph (644–56CE)?

Umar appointed a council of six men to decide his successor, and they chose Uthman, a son-in-law of Muhammad who was from the important Umayyad family of the Quraish tribe. Although he was a deeply religious man (remembered for organising the authoritative version of the Qur'an), he proved to be a weak leader. He allowed members of his own family to take important positions in government, and was held responsible for their bad administration. He became so unpopular that he was eventually assassinated.

Who was Ali (656–61CE)?

The people of Madinah elected Ali as the next caliph. He had a strong claim to the caliphate and had waited 24 years since the Prophet's death for this honour. Ali was the son of Abu Talib, Muhammad's uncle and guardian. He was a lot younger than Muhammad, but had grown up in Muhammad's household, and there was a close, brotherly relationship between the two. He was the next person after Khadijah to believe in Muhammad's prophethood, although only a boy of 10 or 12 at the time. He remained a loyal supporter of Islam ever after. At the Hijrah (see p.31), he risked his life for Muhammad: he slept in the Prophet's bed to fool his enemies into thinking that Muhammad was still there, so giving Muhammad a head start on his pursuers. In Madinah he was a close friend and confidant of the Prophet. He married Muhammad's youngest daughter, Fatimah; and their two sons were the only surviving grandchildren of the Prophet. There are many stories which show Muhammad's fondness for these two boys.

There are Muslims called **Shi'ahs** who believe that Ali was the rightful successor of Muhammad. They refuse to call him the *fourth* caliph, but the first **Imam**, therefore dismissing

the first three caliphates as invalid. Although they look back on this period as a Golden Age, Ali in fact had a difficult time of it. Members of Uthman's family had been made governors all over the empire, and they blamed Ali for his death. Ali tried to restore order by dismissing those in authority whose injustices and inefficiencies had caused unrest during Uthman's caliphate. The powerful governor of Syria, Mu'awiya, refused to recognise Ali as caliph until the assassins had been brought to justice.

Civil war broke out in which Ali proved himself a good soldier, but he eventually made peace. Some of Ali's followers took this as a sign of weakness, demanding that Allah alone should decide the outcome. Ali wasted valuable time and resources dealing with them. They became known as the Kharijites (the 'Seceders') because they were the first to withdraw formally from the other Muslims, forming a separate group within Islam. This puritanical group still exists today, but they never grew into a major movement like the Shi'ah.

It is thought to have been a Kharijite who assassinated Ali in the mosque at Kufa, Iraq in 661. There is some question as to where his remains are buried, but the traditional site is at Najaf in Iraq, which has since become an important religious centre. Among other things, it can boast the world's largest cemetery, surrounding Ali's shrine. The corpses of Shi'ahs from all over the world are brought here, to be taken inside the sanctuary and then carried three times round the outside of Ali's mausoleum, before being buried near to the tombs of Ali and some of the other Imams.

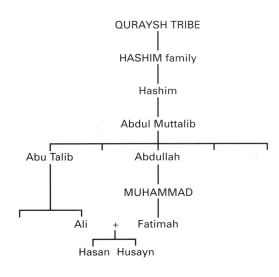

```
              QURAYSH TRIBE
                     |
              HASHIM family
                     |
                  Hashim
                     |
              Abdul Muttalib
         _____|_____
        |            |            |
    Abu Talib     Abdullah
        |            |
        |        MUHAMMAD
        |            |
     ___|___      ___|___
    |                   |
   Ali       +      Fatimah
         ____|____
        |         |
      Hasan     Husayn
```

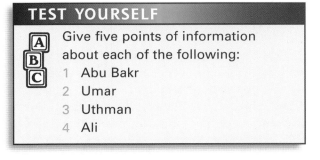

TEST YOURSELF

A B C Give five points of information about each of the following:
1 Abu Bakr
2 Umar
3 Uthman
4 Ali

▲ The golden-domed mosque, Ali's shrine at Najaf in Iraq.

KEY QUESTION

What is Shi'ah Islam?

WHO ARE THE SHI'AHS?

The Shi'ahs are named after the Shi'ah of Ali – the Party of Ali (Shi'ahs believe that Ali was the rightful successor of Muhammad). They can be called **Shi'ahs**, **Shi'is** or **Shi'ites**; and you can talk of Shi'i Islam, Shi'ism or the Shi'ah. The Shi'ahs have always been a minority in Islam, and today they make up about 15 per cent of all Muslims.

The largest group of Shi'ahs (about 62 million) is in Iran, where they form 89 per cent of the population. Iran is the only country to make Shi'ism its official religion. The Iranian Revolution of 1977 was led by a high-ranking religious leader, Ayatollah Khomeini (1902–89), who claimed descent from Muhammad himself (see the photo on p.99). He overthrew the Shah,

the head of state who had westernised the country, and established a government led by the religious leaders, called the 'ulama. They rule the country according to Islamic law, the **Shari'ah**.

The Shi'ahs also form the largest religious group in Iraq, making up 60 per cent of the population. There are also significant Shi'ah minorities in India, Pakistan, the Gulf States, Lebanon and Syria, Russia and East Africa. Virtually all of the remaining 85 per cent of Muslims are **Sunnis** – those who claim to follow the right 'path' of Islam.

TEST YOURSELF

1 What is the meaning of the name 'Sunni'?
2 How did Shi'ism get its name?
3 Who was the only Caliph accepted by both Sunnis and Shi'ahs?

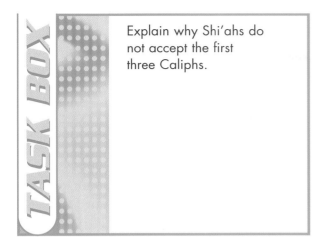

Explain why Shi'ahs do not accept the first three Caliphs.

chosen leader of their community. N.B. Other Muslims use it to describe the prayer-leader at a mosque.)

By this time, Mu'awiya had extended his power so much that he forced Hasan to renounce any claims he had to the caliphate. Freed from opposition, Mu'awiya began the powerful Umayyad Dynasty, which ruled the Islamic empire from Damascus in Syria for about 90 years until 750CE. Hasan retired to Madinah where he lived quietly until his death eight years later.

Why was Husayn, the third Imam (669–80CE), called 'Prince of Martyrs'?

After Hasan's death, his younger brother, Husayn, became head of the House of Ali and, according to Shi'ahs, the third Imam. He knew that there were supporters of the House of Ali in Kufa in Iraq, because there had been a revolt there in 671. The seven leaders who were

What happened to Hasan, the second Imam (661–9CE)?

Shi'ahs regard Ali as the first Imam and believe that, on his death, his authority passed to his eldest son, Hasan, who became the second Imam. (The word imam means a leader, and it is used here by the Shi'ah to denote the divinely

▲ Husayn's shrine in Karbala in Iraq.

executed became the first Shi'ah martyrs. Husayn did nothing until Mu'awiya's death in 680. Then he set out from Arabia with a small army of 72 men, to challenge the authority of Mu'awiya's son, Yazid, at Kufa.

Despite warnings that Yazid's army had a tight hold on Kufa, Husayn pressed onwards. The first detachment of soldiers from Kufa negotiated with him, and he agreed not to march on the city. On 2 Muharram, they encamped on the Plain of Karbala. This first detachment later deserted to Husayn's side, but by this time reinforcements had arrived and cut off their water supply.

By the evening of 9 Muharram, the situation was desperate. Husayn had refused to pledge allegiance to Yazid, and had been refused permission to withdraw. He had only a small army against the enemy's 4000. He had women and children with him, including his sister and two of his sons; and they were all without water. Husayn tried to persuade his men to leave him to face the enemy alone, but they would not hear of it.

On the fateful 10 Muharram AH61 (10 October 680CE, see p. 32), Husayn's men were all killed in battle, and the women and children who survived were taken captive. The Umayyad army returned to Kufa with the heads of Husayn and his followers raised aloft on their spears. Later they took Husayn's head to Yazid in Damascus. It was returned 40 days after his death, to be buried with what remained of his body, where he fell in Karbala. A shrine to Husayn was built there and Karbala in Iraq became an important religious centre. Many Shi'ahs have been buried there.

The massacre at Karbala has had the greatest impact in the history of Shi'ism, which gained momentum from this time. An underground resistance movement was formed in Kufa, called the Penitents – because they were sorry they had not gone to Husayn's aid. In 684CE, 3000 of them revolted and, inspired by the example of Karbala, they were killed in battle against a force of 30,000. This shows the spirit of martyrdom which was to mark the Shi'ah movement.

▲ Men lash their backs with chains. Although these extreme expressions of grieving are not encouraged by the Shi'ah leaders, they are nevertheless a traditional part of the Muharram ceremonies, and some of the devout young men will take part.

How do Shi'ahs commemorate Husayn's death?

The message of Karbala is that Husayn chose death rather than compromise what he believed; and the story of his self sacrifice still moves Shi'ahs to tears and to extreme expressions of grief, as it is commemorated each year. For the first ten days of the month of Muharram, the entire Shi'ah world is plunged into mourning. This comes to a climax on 10 Muharram, the day of 'Ashura (which was a day of fasting long before Husayn's martyrdom). People attend emotional meetings, where Husayn's sufferings are recounted. Women break their glass bangles, a practice that is usually only done when a woman's husband dies. There are also processions, when a replica corpse or coffin is carried through the streets to the sound of chants and drum beats, with the rhythmic beating of breasts or men lashing their backs with chains or cutting their heads with knives. In Shi'ah communities around the world, and particularly in Islamic countries, there are theatrical presentations of the tragedy at Karbala, such as setting fire to 'Husayn's tent'.

The most important city for these commemorations is, of course, Karbala itself, in Iraq. It is traditional for Shi'ah pilgrims from all over the world to gather there for the ten days of Muharram. They perform 'The visitation of Imam Husayn' at his shrine there and join in the processions and prayers. However, under the regime of Saddam Hussein, the Shi'ahs were regarded as a dangerous majority by the Sunnis in power, and they were persecuted. In 1977 the pilgrim march to Karbala was attacked and thereafter the ceremonies were banned. A Shi'ah uprising against the government in 1991 was savagely suppressed and Karbala, including the shrine of Husayn, was wrecked.

The overthrow of Saddam Hussein by Western coalition forces in 2003 meant that Shi'ahs could once more return to Karbala and freely celebrate this festival. Muharram 2004

▲ Atrocities in Karbala – Muharram, 2004.

was therefore a historic celebration of freedom. A million Shi'ah Muslims gathered there, many from abroad. Unfortunately, it became a historic occasion for another more sinister reason. On 10 Muharram, at the height of the ceremonies, six bombs exploded in the procession, killing 270 men, women and children and maiming many others. Similar attacks took place in Baghdad in Iraq and in the Pakistani city of Quetta.

The extremist Islamic organisation, al-Qaeda, was thought to be behind these atrocities because they were so well co-ordinated in different places. Whoever was responsible, it emphasises the historical rift between Sunni and Shi'ah Muslims, kept alive by the Muharram rituals. At this annual festival, Shi'ah Muslims renew their devotion to Imam Husayn, and to a lesser extent his brother Imam Hasan, whom they believe were the divinely appointed leaders of Islam. They also glorify suffering and martyrdom, which has an important part to play in Shi'ah Islam. Shi'ahs claim that all their imams died as martyrs; and the Shi'ahs have often been a persecuted minority within Islam. It was a sign of their determination that, within hours of the devastating bombings in Karbala, the processions and rituals were resumed.

How are the Shi'ah organised?

In the tenth and eleventh centuries CE, Shi'ism achieved political power over almost the whole Islamic world. Then, in the eleventh century, they were severely repressed by the Turks of the Seljuk Dynasty. At the end of the fifteenth century, the Safavid Dynasty came to power in Persia (Iran) and ruled for over 200 years. They became Shi'ah and made it the official religion of Persia.

The main branch of Shi'ism, the Twelvers, or Imamis, are found mostly in Iran today. Their name comes from their belief that their twelfth Imam, called Muhammad, did not die but disappeared. While they await his return, they rely on his representatives to lead them, like the Ayatollahs (meaning 'Sign of Allah').

The next largest group of Shi'ahs is in Lebanon and Syria, and scattered throughout Africa and Asia. They are the Isma'ilis, who accept only seven imams and believe that their seventh imam, called Isma'il, is the Hidden Imam. Their present leader is the Aga Khan, who uses his wealth to fund many charitable organisations through the Aga Khan Development Network. For example, it provides health and education services for the Isma'ilis living in Third World countries.

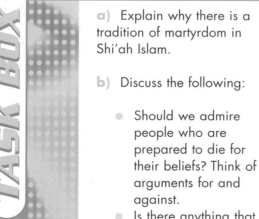

TASK BOX

a) Explain why there is a tradition of martyrdom in Shi'ah Islam.

b) Discuss the following:

- Should we admire people who are prepared to die for their beliefs? Think of arguments for and against.
- Is there anything that you would be prepared to die for?

▲ The Aga Khan.

▲ Ayatollah Khomeini shown on a roadside sign in Beirut, Lebanon. He led the Islamic revolution to victory in Iran in 1977–79. His black turban signifies his descent from the Prophet Muhammad.

Those who accept only seven Imams look for the hidden meaning of the Qur'an in even greater depth than other Shi'ahs, and they have given birth to a number of secretive sects, like the Druze (see the photo on page 100).

The Alawi form another small Shi'ah sect. Their name means 'worshippers of Ali'. They are found in Syria and have combined Islamic beliefs with many others from different religions.

TEST YOURSELF

1 Why do Shi'ahs want to be buried at Najaf and Karbala in Iraq?

2 What do Shi'ahs commemorate at the festival of 'Ashura?

3 Why did the Shi'ah line of Imams come to an end?

4 Name two Shi'ah sects.

▲ The Druze in Israel.

HOW DO SHI'AH AND SUNNI ISLAM DIFFER?

They differ in their leadership:

- Shi'ahs believe that Muhammad chose Ali as his successor. He should therefore have been accepted by all Muslims as the first caliph – or Imam, as they call their leaders. Shi'ahs reject the caliphates of Abu Bakr, Umar and Uthman, and they do not accept any changes implemented by them.
  (N.B. A minority of Shi'ahs, the Zaydis, *do* accept the first three caliphs as well as Ali. These represent the most moderate form of Shi'ism.)
- Shi'ahs believe that each new leader of the Muslim community should be chosen by the previous Imam, by divine inspiration (so that it is really Allah's choice). They also think he should be a descendant of Muhammad, and therefore also of Ali.

- The Sunni caliphs held mainly political power. For the Shi'ahs, their leader's religious authority was far more important. (They could therefore regard Hasan as their Imam, even when he had no political influence.)

They differ in their holy Scriptures:

- Sunnis believe that Muhammad's role in revealing Allah's laws (in the Qur'an) and guiding people to Allah (in the Sunnah) ended with him. Shi'ahs cannot believe that Allah would ever leave them without guidance, and that their leaders have the right to interpret the Qur'an for them. It follows that their Imams must be sinless and unable to make mistakes because Allah would not lead his people astray.

- Sunnis interpret the Qur'an literally, but Shi'ahs claim that its hidden meaning was given by Muhammad to Ali.
- Sunnis accept six books of Hadith which they call 'The Accurate Six'. Shi'ahs have their own collection of books of Hadith, mostly passed on through the Imams.

They differ in the following belief:

- Shi'ahs expect the **Mahdi** (the divinely 'guided' one) to appear before the Day of Judgement, and bring in a reign of justice and peace. This is a popular belief among Sunnis as well; but the Shi'ahs expect the Mahdi to be their Hidden Imam (i.e. their last Imam, whom they believe to have disappeared rather than died).

They differ in some ritual practices:

- All Muslims accept the Five Pillars, but Shi'ahs are permitted to combine the five prayers into three sessions.
- Shi'ahs have many saints. The Twelvers, for instance, venerate the Fourteen Pure Ones (Muhammad, his daughter Fatimah and the Twelve Imams). They perform elaborate rituals at their shrines, and commemorate their births and deaths annually. They also have pictures of their saints, which Sunni Muslims do not allow, for fear of idolatry.

TASK BOX

a) Write a paragraph about the Shi'ah Imams, or list at least 5 points about them from the information given.
b) (Extension.) Find out more about Muslim beliefs in the Mahdi, or about Shi'ah practices at their shrines.

KEY QUESTION
What is Sufism and how important is it in Islam?

WHO ARE THE SUFIS?

The Sufis are Muslims who are not content with *doing* the Five Pillars; they also want to *feel* as close to Allah as possible. They live simple lives, devoting their time and energy to deepening their relationship with Allah. The term **Sufism** appears to go back to the eighth century CE. The early Sufis were individuals who devoted their lives to meditating on the Qur'an. The rough woollen robes which some of them used to wear may have given the name 'Sufism' to this movement in Islam, because *suf* means 'wool'. It was thought that some of the early followers of the Prophet wore simple clothes like this. Sufis look back on the first four caliphs in particular as saintly men who led simple lives, close to Allah; and they try to follow their examples. Sufis today, however, tend to wear conventional clothes except on formal occasions when they may wear special traditional clothes. Alternatively, the name Sufism may come from the Greek *sophos*, meaning 'wisdom', because Sufism helps people to find inner spiritual knowledge.

Since about 870CE, Sufis have been organised into Orders, or Brotherhoods; and these orders became particularly influential in Islam in the twelfth and thirteenth centuries CE. Sufi orders are led by **shaikhs** who hand down their (sometimes secret) teachings to their pupils. Sufis claim that these chains of authority go back to Muhammad himself. Sufis, therefore, follow a religious teacher, and they have to trust themselves to this spiritual guide, putting aside their own ideas and preferences to follow their teacher's advice. There have been a few women heads of Sufi Orders and many women followers recognised as saints. Bibi Rabia (d.801) is a very famous female Sufi saint who was held in great respect by her male contemporaries and continues to be widely revered by men and women alike. The role of being 'mother of a Sufi order', as the wife of a Shaikh is often termed, also carries with it a similar level of respect to the Shaikh.

▲ Whirling Dervishes in Konya, Turkey.

Each Order teaches its own path (**tariqah**), or method of achieving union with Allah. This may be through silent meditation done to rhythmic breathing, or through rhythmic chanting, or dance (even though mainstream Islam rejects music and dance in its religion). The most famous method is that of the Mevlevi in Turkey, founded by Jalal ud-din Rumi (1207–73CE) in Konya in Turkey. He became the greatest religious poet of Persia (modern Iran), possibly of all Islam, and his followers are popularly known as the Dancing or Whirling Dervishes. In a sacred dance accompanied by musicians, each dervish spins round and round whilst moving slowly around the room, with one hand raised to heaven and the other pointing down to the earth, trying to become a channel of communication between the two. Their dancing is carefully controlled, and when the music stops, they form up and file out in an orderly way. The ceremony begins and ends with recitation of the holy Qur'an, as do all formal Sufi ceremonies.

TEST YOURSELF

1. What is most important to Sufis?
2. Where is their name likely to have come from?
3. What is the head of a Sufi Order called?
4. Name a female Sufi saint.
5. Who was the founder of the Mevlevi Order?
6. What is the Mevlevi Order particularly known for?

WHO WAS AL-GHAZALI (1059–111CE)?

Al-Ghazali was one of the greatest scholars of Islam, and he helped to make Sufism acceptable within Islam. He was a brilliant professor in Baghdad in Iraq until his late thirties, when he became more and more dissatisfied with intellectual knowledge alone. After a six-month struggle with his feelings, in desperation he gave up his position at the university, left behind his family, and went to Syria where he lived the simple life of a Sufi. After two years, he made the pilgrimage to Makkah and then returned home to support his family. From then on he practised **Sufism**, which had a great influence on his later writings. He will always be remembered for *The Revival of the Religious Sciences*, which is the greatest theological book in Islam. He taught that the external practices of religion need to go hand-in-hand with personal, inner religious faith. Despite his own intellect and learning, he defended the religious devotion of the humble, uneducated Muslim. He thought that Sufism was one way of approaching Allah, but he rejected its claim to have a special, hidden truth of its own. At first he was criticised by the religious leaders of his day, but gradually his message was accepted and he became revered as a saint. Just as great Medieval thinkers like Aquinas still influence Catholic belief, so al-Ghazali still influences Islam.

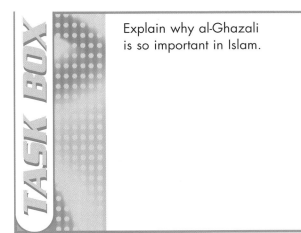

Explain why al-Ghazali is so important in Islam.

WHAT DOES THE CONFERENCE OF THE BIRDS TEACH?

Sufi teachings are often difficult to understand, because the idea is that they should be experienced rather than just studied (just as you can read about love, but you will never fully understand it until you are in love). Sufis often put across their ideas in stories, because the listener can enter imaginatively into the story and experience something of its meaning. A famous Sufi story from the twelfth century CE is the Conference of the Birds. It tells how birds were called to undertake a long and hazardous journey to find the king bird. Not all of them responded to the call, and many disappeared on the way as they met with difficulties and dangers. Only 30 managed to complete the journey and reach their king. When they did, they discovered that they were no longer 30 separate birds, but they were all part of the king bird.

This story has a deep meaning: the king bird represents Allah, and the journey is the spiritual journey each person is called to make in life. A Western Sufi says of it:

> The spiritual interpretation is immensely deeper and richer … It seems to me to rest on the basis of the journey towards God and the recognition (not merely by the intellect) that the journey is, and always was, 'within God'. I cannot give adequate expression to the depth, breadth, and height of this book.

Jamil Morris

a) What do you think this story teaches about the spiritual journey towards God? Consider: Why do people shy away from starting out on this journey? Why do some people give up on the way? What do those who complete the journey discover about themselves and God?
b) Why might mainstream Islam be offended by this teaching about God?

The following two extracts are taken from *Alive to God, Muslim and Christian Prayer* by Kenneth Cragg (pp.81 and 92). The first is a poem by an Egyptian Sufi master of the thirteenth century CE. In this poem, how does al-Dirini think of God?

> My God and my Lord, eyes are at rest, stars are setting, hushed
> are the movements of birds in their nests, of monsters in the deep. [...]
> The doors are locked, watched by their bodyguards.
> But thy door is open to him who calls on thee.
> My Lord, each lover is now alone with his beloved.
> Thou for me art the beloved One.
>
> *'Abd al-'Aziz al-Dirini; Purity of Heart*

The next extract is from a prayer of the Naqshabandi Order of Sufis, which was founded in Persia in the fourteenth century CE by Baha' al-Din Naqshabandi. The Naqshabandi is now the largest Sufi order worldwide. Find the four words in the opening part of the prayer that describe God.

> O my God, how gentle art thou with him who has transgressed against thee: how near thou art to him who seeks thee, how tender to him who petitions thee, how kindly to him who hopes in thee.
>
> Who is he who asked of thee and thou didst deny him, or who sought refuge in thee and thou didst betray him, or drew near to thee and thou didst hold him aloof, or fled unto thee and thou didst repulse him?

HOW IMPORTANT IS SUFISM TODAY?

Sufism has influenced both Sunni and Shi'ah Islam and has helped to spread Islam, especially in Africa and now in the West. It has sometimes met with disapproval and opposition because its beliefs were thought to be heretical, but more often it has been tolerated and recognised as a valid part of Islam. Some regard Sufism as having saved Islam from being too concerned with rules and outward rituals, by emphasising the inner meaning of Islamic practices. Many Westerners in Europe and the USA have been attracted to Islam through Sufism because of its emphasis on inner spiritual experiences and its message of love for all and service of fellow human beings. Sufis believe that we are all united under God, and therefore they respect other religions.

Today, Sufism is found not only in the Sufi Orders but also in its more general influence on popular religious worship. One example of this is **dhikr**, the 'remembrance' of Allah through the repetition of his names. Phrases like *Allahu Akbar* and *La ilaha illallah* are frequently on Muslims' lips; and others such as *Subhanallah*, which means 'Glory be to Allah', and *Al hamdu lilla*, which means 'All praise be to Allah'. The use of prayer beads to count off the number of repetitions also comes from Sufism. Muslims believe that dhikr will bring them closer to Allah and help them to keep his commandments.

ARE THERE SUFIS IN BRITAIN?

Only a small minority of Muslims in Britain are members of a Sufi Order, though many more are probably sympathetic to Sufi ideas, and it does appeal to Western converts. The main Sufi orders in Britain are the Naqshabandi, the biggest order worldwide; the Chishti, an ascetic order whose followers take a vow of poverty; and the Qadiri Order, which is the most widespread worldwide and is found especially among Pakistani Muslims in Britain. These are broken down into many sub-divisions with their own Sufi saints. One such saint is Dr Zahurul Hassan Sharib who died in 1996 and whose body lies buried near the shrine of Chishti in Ajmer, India. These are some of his teachings, spoken at a meeting in Holland in 1983, explaining the importance of Sufism for our modern world.

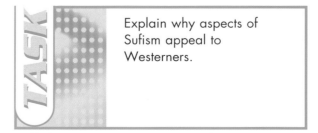

TASK

Explain why aspects of Sufism appeal to Westerners.

A New Approach – Islam

▲ A Sufi Muslim in Kenya praying at the tomb of the great teacher Habib Salih.

PERSPECTIVES

Knowledge is of various kinds. To take a degree from a university or to read a book is an ordinary thing ... But Sufi saints rely more on a different source of knowledge, which is given to a very few. Which comes as a gift of God. That source is intuition and inspiration and they rely upon it. ...

When your radio is on, then you can have news from some city. Though there is news every time, but if your radio set is closed and the switch is not on you cannot hear it. As soon as it is on, you can hear some news, some music, some message. So is the heart of man. If it is calm and tranquil you can get the message, you can hear the voice, and you can be guided by the light. But if there is inner disturbance, confusion, chaos, turmoil, then all those outlets which receive the message, they are closed. ...

Modern man, in spite of all that he has achieved, is devoid of inner peace. And this inner peace – people have longed to achieve it, in whatever direction (it can be found). Taking this in view, I think Sufism has a bright prospect. This century – I mean the twentieth century – is marked as an age of strife. Here the law is get on or get out. ... But Sufism teaches that those who cannot get on should be enabled to get on, and they should not be asked to get out. This means there is a spirit of accommodation, there is a spirit of reconciliation, ... and there is a spirit of mutual help. By these virtues inherent in Sufism people are being drawn towards it, and it is spreading in the West, as it was spreading in the East in the last century ...

Quoted by permission of Jamil Morris from The Zahuri Sufi Web Site, www.zahuri.org, March 2004

A twenty-first-century Western follower of this saint, named Jamiluddin Morris Zahuri, expresses his religious insights in poetry such as this one, entitled 'With Thy Love'.

> By Thy signs inform me,
> With Thy arms enfold me,
> To Thy breast hold me,
> With Thy love destroy me.
>
> By Thy hand take me,
> With Thy fragrance drown me,
> By Thy look absorb me,
> With Thy love destroy me.
>
> By Thy Grace enchant me,
> With Thy thought control me,
> By Thy lip imbibe me,
> With Thy love destroy me.
>
> By Thy beauty excite me,
> With Thy presence pervade me, ·
> By Thy union calm me,
> With Thy love destroy me.

Quoted by permission of Jamil Morris from The Zahuri Sufi Web Site, www.zahuri.org, March 2004

TASK BOX

a) To whom is the poet speaking (notice 'Thy' has a capital T)?
b) What Sufi ideas about God and the Sufi's relationship with God are expressed in this poem?
c) Discuss the following: Do you think Sufism has made an important contribution to Islam, or has it introduced ideas and practices that detract from mainstream Islam?
Give examples to support your answer.

KEY QUESTION
Where is Islam to be found today?

WHERE IS ISLAM ESTABLISHED IN THE WORLD TODAY?

Islam is now the second biggest religion in the world, after Christianity. The maps show that Islam has spread throughout the world. There are over 42 Muslim countries (the smaller Gulf States, for example, are not shown on Map B). The total world population of Muslims is estimated at around 1,300 million.

Although Muhammad lived in Arabia, most Muslims today are not Arabs. They include Africans and Asians as well as Western converts. There are over 2 million Muslims in Britain, which is about 2.7 per cent of the population. But the countries that are almost entirely Muslim are mainly those to which Islam originally spread from Arabia: along the north coast of Africa to Egypt, Libya, Tunisia, Algeria and Morocco; and to the countries of the Middle East such as Jordan, Iraq, Iran and Afghanistan. Islam spread to other parts of Africa and to Indonesia in South Asia in the twentieth century. Indonesia now has the highest Muslim population, of 180 million, followed by Pakistan with 148.5 million. There are well over 100 million Muslims in India and also in Bangladesh, well over 60 million each in Turkey, Egypt, Iran and Nigeria, and over 30 million each in China and Algeria.

Of all the Muslim countries, Turkey has done most to westernise its laws. At the other extreme, Saudi Arabia, Pakistan and Iran have strictly adhered to Shari'ah laws and applied them most widely. Iran is the only country to make Shi'ah Islam the state religion.

(To check on population figures and Muslim percentages of any country, you can ask in the Reference Section of your local library for the current edition of The Statesman's Year-Book, published annually by Palgrave Macmillan.)

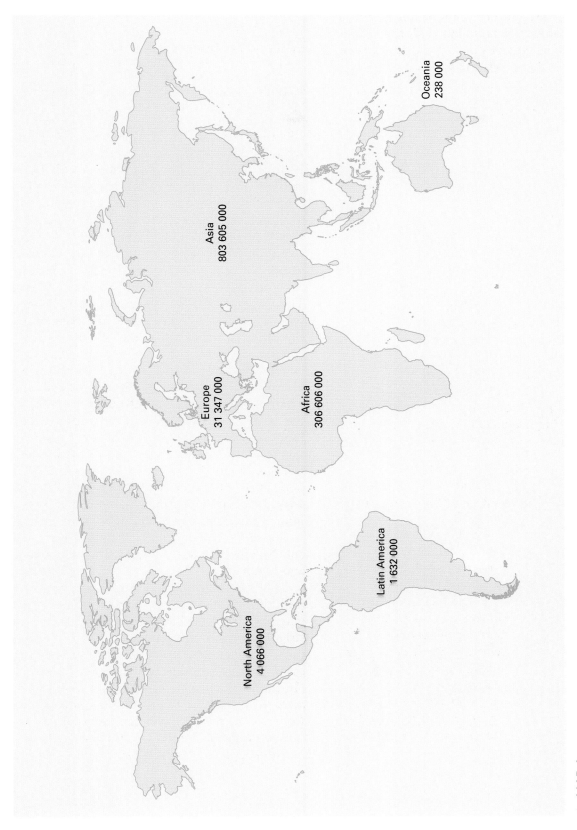

Oceania
238 000

Asia
803 605 000

Europe
31 347 000

Africa
306 606 000

North America
4 066 000

Latin America
1 632 000

▲ MAP A
World distribution of Islam by six continental areas, mid-1997. (Figures, to the nearest thousand, are taken from *World Christian Encylopedia*, Second Edition, OUP.)

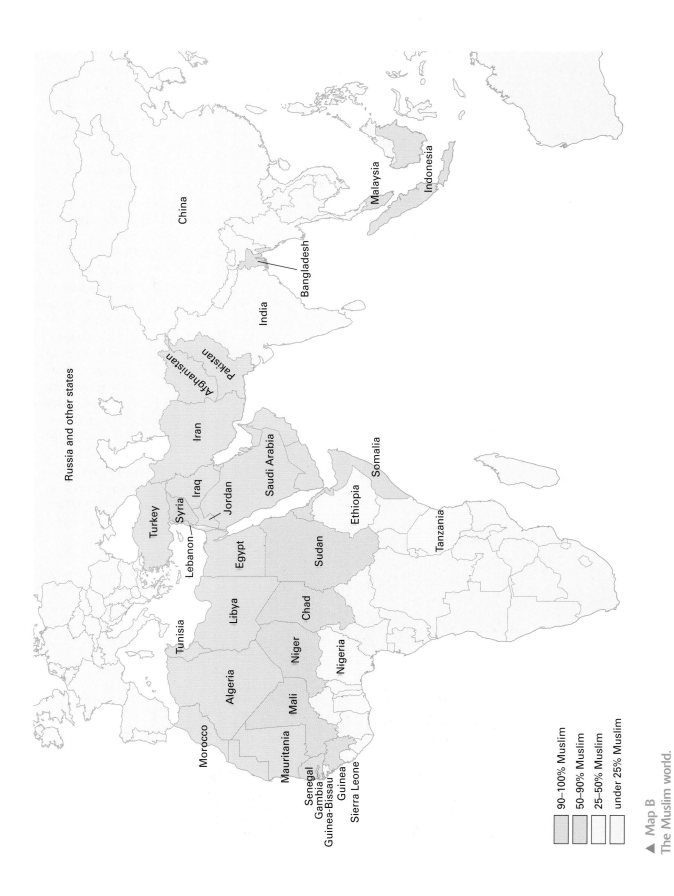

China

Russia and other states

Malaysia

Indonesia

Bangladesh

India

Afghanistan

Pakistan

Iran

Saudi Arabia

Somalia

Iraq

Jordan

Ethiopia

Turkey

Syria

Tanzania

Lebanon

Egypt

Sudan

Tunisia

Libya

Chad

Niger

Nigeria

Algeria

Mali

Mauritania

Morocco

Senegal

Gambia

Guinea-Bissau

Guinea

Sierra Leone

90–100% Muslim

50–90% Muslim

25–50% Muslim

under 25% Muslim

▲ Map B
The Muslim world.

A New Approach – Islam

WHAT IS IT LIKE IN A COUNTRY RUN BY MUSLIM LAWS?

Bearing in mind that Islamic countries have different cultural traditions, let us take Saudi Arabia as an example of a Muslim state. The Arabian House of Saud has been associated with the Wahhabi Islamic movement since it began with 'Abd-al-Wahhab in the eighteenth century CE. He preached a return to the Shari'ah, i.e. laws based on the Qur'an and the **Sunnah**. The Wahhabis are puritanical, in that they disapprove of all frivolity like music, dancing and the wearing of gold by men; they are highly moral and live simple lives. They are opposed to any social mixing of men and women in public (even shaking hands), and would prefer women to stay in the confines of their homes. In religious practices, they emphasise the oneness of Allah above all else and are therefore strongly against the veneration of saints and the building of their shrines. Their mosques are plain and simple.

The House of Saud unified Arabia in the Kingdom of Saudi Arabia in 1932. This was on the wave of the Wahhabi revival, so we should expect to find Islam strictly enforced there. The King is both the political and religious leader but, although he is individually very powerful, he must act within the Shari'ah, if he wishes to retain his support. In 1964, for example, King Saud was forced to abdicate by the 'People Who Bind and Loose', an organisation of senior princes, 'ulama notables, and government leaders who safeguard the Shari'ah.

The two holiest sites of Islam are situated in Saudi Arabia – at Makkah and Madinah. The King is the guardian of these sites and his government accommodates the millions of pilgrims who come there from all over the world. He is therefore an important leader for the Islamic world, as well as for Saudi Arabia, and has given foreign aid to poorer Islamic states like Pakistan and to Muslim communities abroad.

Oil revenue plunged Saudi Arabia into the modern technological revolution (particularly since 1970, when oil prices began to rise dramatically). Oil production meant that the country needed a skilled and educated workforce, and its revenue provided the money for development. The monarch had to lead his country into modernisation, without betraying its basic Islamic principles. Saudi Arabia is therefore a curious mixture of the ancient and the modern. Its capital city, Riyadh, has impressive modern buildings spreading out beyond what

▲ King Fahd of Saudi Arabia (in 2002).

remains of the old mud-walled city. Education now includes more secular than religious subjects; but modern radio and television are used for a lot of religious education. Girls now make up about half the primary and secondary school population; but there is strict segregation of the genders at all levels. Some women go on to higher education; but they have to be taken to and from college by a male member of their family, since women are forbidden to drive or travel alone. Women are now allowed to appear on television, to read the news and present children's programmes – as long as they are not Saudi women.

▲ The modern city of Riyadh, capital of Saudi Arabia.

A New Approach – Islam

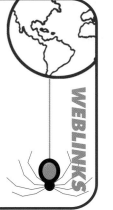

Use a search engine (e.g. www.google.co.uk) to find out more about any Muslim country.

WEBLINKS

1 a) Describe the differences between Sunni and Shi'ah Muslims.

b) Explain how Sufi practices help them to feel close to God.

c) Do you think diversity within a religion strengthens or weakens it? Consider different points of view and refer to Islam in your answer.

Assignment

Growing Up in Islam

8

KEY WORDS

aqiqah: birth ceremonies.
Bismillah: 'In the name of Allah, the Merciful, the Compassionate'.
fard: obligatory.
halal: permitted.
haram: forbidden.
khitan: circumcision.
madrasah: religious school.
mahr: wedding dowry.
Salat al-Janazah: the funeral prayer.
Shari'ah: Islamic law.

KEY QUESTION

How does Islam affect a Muslim's way of life?

WHAT HAPPENS WHEN A BABY IS BORN TO A MUSLIM FAMILY?

▲ The newborn baby hears the call to prayer.

The call to prayer

Islam is a religion that affects the whole of a Muslim's life on earth, every day of their lives from birth to death. Islam teaches that this life on earth is our chance to prepare for the life to come. It is therefore supremely precious.

When a Muslim baby is born, his father, another man of the family, or the local imam, speaks the call to prayer (see pp.16–17) into the baby's ears. The adhan is spoken into the right ear, and the 'iqamah into the left. This is done as soon as possible after birth.

Although the child cannot yet understand these words, the ceremony introduces the child to its religion and shows that the parents want to bring it up within Islam. Muslims believe that babies are born pure and free from sin, but that they lack knowledge and experience. It is therefore very important for Muslims that they guide them in the right way.

Muslims believe that, by following Islam, they are living in the way God intended us all to live. Islam teaches that all of us are born Muslims, because we naturally 'submit' to God's laws. They believe, therefore, that all who die in childhood will enjoy the rewards of Muslims in heaven, since it is only as we grow up that we can cease to be Muslims, either by ignoring God or by choosing to follow another religion. Muslims therefore place great importance on encouraging their children to continue within Islam.

▲ The baby's head is shaved.

Shaving the head

The **aqiqah** ceremony usually takes place when the baby is seven days old. Passages from the Qur'an are recited, and a number of special rituals are performed.

The baby's hair is shaved off and weighed. Traditionally, its weight in gold or silver is given to the poor. Today, parents usually give a donation of whatever they can afford to charity. In many cultures, hair is regarded as unclean. Shaving off the hair is therefore a symbol of purity. The child is regarded as a gift and blessing from Allah. One way of saying 'Thank you' for this most precious gift is to give something in return – to be used by those who need it most.

▲ The child is named.

Naming the child

The child is then named. Customs vary as to who in the family is given the privilege of choosing the name: often it is the grandfather, otherwise it is the parents who choose. Names are usually chosen to honour great Muslims from the past. So a boy might be named after the Prophet Ibrahim, or the Caliph Umar. A girl might be named after Muhammad's wife Ayesha, or his daughter Fatimah. Many boys are given the name Muhammad, although they might well be known by a second name, to save the confusion of so many boys having the same name. Another tradition is to give boys one of the 99 names of Allah from the Qur'an, such as Halim, which means 'patient'. When this is done, it always has the word *'Abd* in front of it, which means 'servant' (e.g. 'Abd al-Halim). In the same way, they would never call anyone Allah, but Abdullah is a common Muslim name, meaning 'Servant of Allah'.

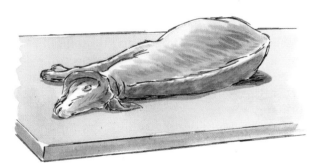

▲ There is an animal sacrifice.

Animal sacrifice

It is traditional to sacrifice two sheep or goats for a boy, and one for a girl. Like the sacrifice at Id-ul-Adha, this is done by a halal butcher in Western countries, and a third of the meat is eaten, another third given to friends and relatives, and another third given to the poor. People share food together to celebrate happy occasions, providing the best food that they can afford. At all Muslim festivals, people want to share their good fortune with those who are less fortunate in life. Although Muhammad did much to improve the situation of women, men continued to take a dominant role in Muslim society. Therefore there is particular rejoicing over the birth of a boy.

▲ A baby boy is circumcised.

Circumcision

Boys are circumcised in Islam (as in Judaism); it is called **khitan** in Arabic. This is often done at the aqiqah ceremony, or at 21 days, or even when the child is older. A Muslim doctor performs the simple operation (cutting off the foreskin) after a prayer is said.

Muslims continue to do this today because it is a religious practice which was started by the Prophet Ibrahim.

Other Customs

You may come across many birth customs among Muslim families other than those described here. Sometimes they have come from other cultures rather than from Islamic teachings. A few of the customs are superstitious and are frowned upon by some Muslims. One example is the tying of a black thread around the baby's wrist to ward off the Evil Eye. Other customs express the common human desire to mark special stages in the baby's life, like the first time it eats solid food, and its first birthday.

TEST YOURSELF

1 What is the first religious ceremony when a Muslim baby is born?
2 What is done with the hair that is shaved off the young baby's head?
3 Give three Muslim names and explain their significance.
4 How many sheep or goats are killed for a feast when a Muslim boy is born?
5 What is khitan and why is it done?

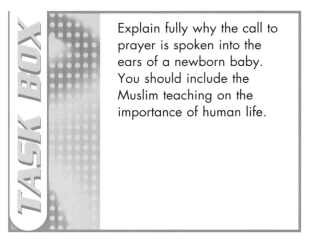

TASK BOX

Explain fully why the call to prayer is spoken into the ears of a newborn baby. You should include the Muslim teaching on the importance of human life.

HOW DO MUSLIM CHILDREN LEARN THE TEACHINGS OF ISLAM?

Just as it is important for Muslim parents to set their children off on the right road at birth, so it is important to continue to bring them up in the Islamic faith.

A Muslim's whole life is governed by **Shari'ah**, the Islamic law, which literally means the 'straight path'. Muslims must therefore know what is obligatory (**fard**), for example, the Five Pillars; what is permitted (**halal**); and what is forbidden (**haram**) to them. The Shari'ah is based on the Qur'an and the Sunnah; so children will gradually learn to read the Qur'an, and will be told stories about Muhammad, as examples for them to follow. The Shari'ah is arrived at by the common consent (ijma) of Islamic scholars. Where neither the Qur'an nor the Sunnah give direct rules, the method of analogy is used. Scholars find a similar issue on which there is some teaching and apply the same principle to the new situation. For example, the killing of infants is forbidden in the Qur'an so now abortion is forbidden. The Shari'ah encompasses both public and private life. It has laws that you would expect to be made by the political authorities, as well as rules for areas of life which might be regarded as private morality. It teaches Muslims how Allah wants them to live the whole of their lives. Since Islam affects the whole of life, children gradually learn their religion at home and at school.

The Bismillah in Arabic. ▲

▲ These Muslim girls learn about their religion at classes held out of school hours at their mosque.

Some Muslim countries have Arabic as their language, but if this is not the case, it is important for Muslim children to become familiar with the Arabic in the Qur'an and used in their worship. The first phrase they learn is the **Bismillah**: *Bismillah ir Rahman ir Rahim* (In the name of Allah, the Compassionate, the Merciful). This is the opening of all but one of the surahs in the Qur'an, and is frequently used by Muslims. Some Muslims have a special celebration, with presents, when a child can recite it. This may be part of the child's fourth birthday celebrations, if the family remember birthdays (which is not done in every culture).

From then on, children will attend the **madrasah**. This is a religious school run by the mosque. In Islamic countries, it could be an ordinary day school. In Western countries it is usually run after day school or sometimes at the weekend. Children are taught Islamic beliefs, how to pray, and how to read the Qur'an.

There is no set time laid down in the Qur'an for coming of age in Islam. Nor is there a special ceremony for this. Muslim children will gradually learn their religion through practice, as they grow up. By about the age of seven, they will be doing the five daily prayers. By ten, they will probably be doing some daily fasts, but not yet for the whole month of Ramadan. By the time they have reached puberty, they must accept the obligations of the Five Pillars, if they are to continue to be Muslims. Some Muslim countries count this as the age of 12. At about this age, a Muslim child usually finishes learning to recite the Qur'an, and the family celebrate this event.

> Amr bin Shu'aib narrated on the authority of his father who narrated from his father that the Messenger of Allah (peace and blessing of Allah be upon him) said: Command your children to offer prayer when they attain the age of seven, and when they attain the age of ten and do not observe prayer, then force them to do so. And separate them in their beds.

Sunan Abu Dawud; Selection from Hadith, No.17, p.11

This article celebrates the success of Muslim students in one London secondary school for boys.

Rukhsana Sheikh, senior vice-principal, said: 'We have made Muslims feel valued and raised pupil and parental aspirations by showing what each student was capable of achieving.'

The school gives Muslim boys access to a prayer room at lunch time, halal food and trips to the local mosque every Friday. Boys and girls in the mixed sixth-form can wear traditional dress. There are regular lessons and assemblies on all religions ...

Times Educational Supplement 10 October 2003 'Model for Muslim success'

There is naturally much concern about the education of Muslim children living in the West. Most go to ordinary local schools where they hope that their beliefs will be respected. Muslims are particularly worried about such things as the provision of halal meat at school dinners; permission for Muslim girls to wear traditional dress (e.g. head scarves and loose trousers to cover their legs); and separate PE and swimming lessons for boys and girls. There were protests by Muslims, in 2004, when the French government banned the wearing of headscarves and other conspicuous religious symbols in their schools.

Many Muslims living in non-Muslim countries would prefer their children to be educated in Islamic schools, but there are relatively few of these. In the UK, the first private Muslim school, the London School of Islamics, was set up in 1981. By 2002, there were 102 such schools, educating approximately 10,000 Muslim pupils. This leaves the majority with no choice but to attend state schools. The government's inspection of schools indicated in 2004 that the British state system often failed to meet the needs of Muslim pupils and their parents. There was a need for special Islamic classes, more single-sex education, prayer rooms in secondary schools and religious awareness training for staff and governors. In 1998, the first government grants were given to two Islamic primary schools in Britain (in the same way as Church schools are supported). In 2000, this was extended to secondary schools, when the first Muslim secondary school was given the go-ahead in Bradford. But this is a slow process and by 2002 there were still only four Muslim state schools. Dr Baig, headmaster of the Islamic Primary School in Brent (West London), explains how Islamic schools are special:

We want to educate the children with a thorough understanding of the Islamic faith and its importance, and to this end we use part of every day to teach Islamic studies. But we are also concerned with creating an atmosphere, a way of behaving which is in line with the restraint, the respect for elders, the obedience which is something Muslims believe to be very important.

The Times Educational Supplement

TASK BOX

Discuss the following:

Do you think it is good for Muslims to be educated in Islamic schools?
Give arguments for and against.

▲ A Halal food shop in the UK.

Muslims must only eat halal food (which means 'permitted' according to Islamic laws, as opposed to haram which means 'forbidden'). All fish and vegetables are permitted, alcohol is forbidden, and there are some restrictions on meat.

Muslims are forbidden to eat any product from the pig. They are also forbidden to eat the meat of any animals which have died (and not been slaughtered). Other animals must be killed according to Islamic regulations before their meat is permitted. The animal's throat must be cut swiftly with a sharp knife, and the Bismillah blessing said over it. Muslims believe this is the most painless way of killing an animal, and it allows the blood to drain away.

Muslims are taught not to waste their food because it comes from Allah the Creator. They should take only as much food as they can eat. At the end of a meal, if there are leftovers which cannot be re-used, they are thrown out for the birds rather than being wasted.

TASK BOX

a) If you wanted to serve meat to a Muslim, what would you have to consider?

b) List at least five foods that are forbidden to Muslims because they come from pigs (remember that lard, made from pork fat, is used in many products).

c) Explain why Muslims disapprove of wasting food.

HOW SHOULD MUSLIMS DRESS?

There is much emphasis in Islam on respect for the opposite sex, and particularly on the protection of women from men's sexual desires. So Muslim society does not approve of nudity, and as children grow up they are taught to be discreet about their bodies. Once boys reach puberty, they must cover themselves at least from the navel to the knees. Girls must cover their tops as well, but do not have to cover their heads, necks and arms when they are at home or in all-female company.

Outside the home, Muslim women usually cover up much more than this, depending on what is acceptable in the societies where they live. Modesty is the main consideration in dress for both sexes. Women should wear loose clothing that does not show off their figures, and the material should be thick enough not to be seen through. Women will also cover their hair and sometimes parts of their face. In strict Islamic countries, like Saudi Arabia, Pakistan and Iran, women must be fully veiled from head to toe. It is mostly a matter of the interpretation of Qur'anic passages like these:

> Tell believing women to avert their glances and guard their private parts, and not to display their charms except what (normally) appears of them.
>
> *Qur'an 24:30 (The Qur'an Basic Teachings, p.206)*

> Remain in your homes and do not (publicly) display your beauty in the way they used to do during (the time of) primitive ignorance.
>
> *Qur'an 33:33 (The Qur'an. Basic Teachings, p.206)*

Apart from modesty, another consideration is simplicity. Muslims are generally against wearing clothes which show off their wealth. Nor are women allowed to wear male dress or vice versa, because of the sexual deviancy that this implies. Men are forbidden to wear silk and pure gold.

TASK BOX

Discuss the following:

a) Islamic dress rules are based on modesty. Do you think this is a good guiding principle, or not? What rules govern the clothes that you wear, and can you think of better ones?

b) What difficulties face Muslim teenagers living in a non-Muslim country like Britain? What are the main reasons for these difficulties? What could be done in schools to help them?

PERSPECTIVES

There is a lot of misunderstanding between Muslims and non-Muslim Westerners over the purpose of Islamic dress regulations. Yet it seems that most Muslims, both men and women, are in favour of Islamic dress because it gives women respect. The Chairman of The Islamic Society for the Promotion of Religious Tolerance in the UK says this:

Protected in her own symbol of dignity (her dress) the woman can feel free to take whichever role in her society that she wishes to do, without the added burden of having to constantly look beautiful (more artificially than naturally) or having to succumb to the temptation of being used for ornamental beautification of streets and offices. The unspoken 'jargon' of the Moslem dress is really to say to the man: 'Hey, stop looking at my own private body and look at my mind instead!'

Hesham El Essawy, letter of 25 September 1984

WHAT IS DISTINCTIVE ABOUT MUSLIM MARRIAGE?

Muslim boys and girls do not have the same opportunities to mix as do Western teenagers, and therefore marriages are usually arranged by the parents. While boys are allowed to play out on the streets, a closer eye is kept on Muslim girls. Once they reach puberty, boys and girls are not allowed to mix freely together outside their homes. This means that Western-style teenage parties and clubs are frowned upon; and Muslim girls will tend to make their own social lives within their homes. Obviously, this is done to prevent promiscuity. Islam teaches that the right and only place for sex is within marriage. This does not mean that Islam is against sex. On the contrary, it regards sex as a natural part of being human and therefore as a gift from Allah. But, if people are to benefit from sex, it must be used in the way Allah intended, and not abused. So Muslims are encouraged to marry young.

TASK BOX

Discuss the following:

Islam teaches that the right place for sex is within marriage. How do you think Muslim parents would defend this either to their son or to their daughter? Do you agree? Give reasons for your points of view.

Arranged marriage is common practice in Islam (as it is for two-thirds of the world's population), although this is not laid down in the Qur'an, and no one should be forced into marrying against his or her will. A boy's parents will look out for a suitable partner for their son, and will approach the girl's parents before she is asked for her consent. Reasons can be put forward both for and against arranged marriages, but most people seem to prefer whatever is the accepted social norm. Generally, difficulties only arise where there are conflicting ideas within society, for example, for Muslims growing up in the West.

> It is not always harmful for the young to benefit from the experience of their loving parents, who usually look for compatible partners rather than the short-lived romantic ones ... Some western girls, incidentally, confess to being secretly envious of arranged marriages as at least it lessens the risk of growing old in loneliness, as well as freeing them from having to kiss so many frogs before they find a prince!

Hesham El Essawy, letter of 30 October 1984

In arranged marriages, the couple have to grow to love the one they marry, rather than marry the one they love, but this still produces loving relationships which are often more stable than their Western counterparts. The tenderness and love experienced between husband and wife are seen as part of Allah's intentions for men and women, as this passage from the Qur'an shows:

> And of His signs is that He created for you, of yourselves, spouses, that you might repose in them, and He has set between you love and mercy.

Qur'an 30:20 (Arberry)

Part of the arrangements include coming to an agreement about the dowry, called the **mahr**. This is a sum of money paid by the bridegroom to the bride, as a token of his appreciation of her. Officially it belongs to the wife to do with as she pleases. In practice it is often paid before the marriage to help towards the wedding expenses and setting up the newly-weds in their home. It is sometimes paid partly in goods. There is another delayed dowry, the amount of which is stated clearly on the wedding certificate. This is not paid unless the couple get divorced or the husband dies (it is taken from the estate before distributing it among those who are entitled to inherit from the deceased). This gives the woman some measure of financial security.

List and discuss arguments for and against arranged marriage.

What happens at a Muslim wedding?

Wedding ceremonies differ considerably from one Muslim society to another, and it is not proposed to describe any in detail here. The following information refers to Muslim marriages that are not restricted by non-Muslim laws.

- The wedding may take place anywhere, and is often in the home or the mosque (but not the worship hall).
- Strictly speaking, the only people necessary are the bride, groom and two adult witnesses. In practice, the local imam is often asked to officiate, and the bride may choose her father to speak for her. Close relatives will also be there, with many other guests from family and friends.
- The essential part of an Islamic wedding is the solemn contract. The bride and groom must agree to this and sign it. It is also signed by the two witnesses. The words will be something like this:

The father of the bride:
'I marry you my daughter according to Allah's book, the Holy Qur'an and the Sunnah of the Messenger of Allah (PBUH) with the dowry agreed upon.'

The bridegroom replies:
'I accept marrying you myself, according to Allah's Book, the Qur'an and the Sunnah of the Messenger of Allah (PBUH) and with the dowry agreed upon.'

ICC leaflet by Dr Sayyed Darsh

Prayers may be said for Allah's blessing on the marriage, and passages from the Qur'an recited. Celebrations follow, according to custom, with many traditions to wish the couple good luck in their new life together. There will be a marriage feast for all the guests (but without alcohol).

▲ A Muslim couple get married in New York.

What is married life like for the bride and groom?

The bride will go to live with her husband and his family. It is the husband's responsibility to protect and provide for his wife (since many Muslims believe a woman's biological make-up may mean that any career she has will be restricted by child-bearing). With a man's responsibilities comes also a certain measure of privilege, laid down in the Qur'an:

> Men are the ones who support women since God has given some persons advantages over others, and because they spend their wealth (on them).
>
> *Qur'an 4:34*
>
> Women have the same (rights in relation to their husbands) as are expected in all decency from them; while men stand a step above them.
>
> *Qur'an 2:228 (The Qur'an. Basic Teachings, p.202)*

So the husband has the final say in all major decisions, even though the wife will have a lot of influence in the home. Muslims believe that this is necessary for an orderly existence, but in practice it usually means that the wife has to do a lot of giving.

Muslim couples are encouraged to have children, as this is natural and is therefore seen to be in accordance with Allah's laws. It is also considered natural for women to bring up the children; many Muslim women do not work outside the home. Contraception is not generally encouraged, but most Muslim societies permit its use because Muhammad allowed contraception if there was a good reason for it. The family might not be able to afford any more children or the mother's health might be at risk. Abortion, on the other hand, is strictly forbidden in Islam, except in rare cases where the mother's life is endangered. Children are considered a blessing from Allah, and to terminate a pregnancy would be regarded as killing a life which Allah has given.

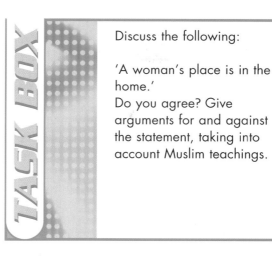

TASK BOX

Discuss the following:

'A woman's place is in the home.'
Do you agree? Give arguments for and against the statement, taking into account Muslim teachings.

Is it true that Muslim men can have a number of wives?

According to Islamic teaching, men are allowed to marry up to four wives; but women may only have one husband. Muhammad himself is said to have had 12 wives during the last part of his life, although he was married to Khadijah alone for the first 24 years of his married life. In Muhammad's time, polygamy was a good way of providing for the widows, when many young husbands were killed in battle.

Today, polygamy is not very common among Muslims, for a number of reasons. The first wife can write a clause into the marriage contract, insisting that she should remain the only wife. Polygamy is expensive, not only to keep a number of wives, but also to pay their dowries. Also, the Qur'an advises men to have only one wife unless they can be sure to treat all their wives equally (which is virtually impossible):

> ... then marry such women as may seem good to you, two or three or four (at a time). If you fear that you will not act justly, then (marry) one woman (only) or someone your right hand controls. That is more likely to keep you from committing an injustice.
>
> *Qur'an 4:3*
>
> You will never manage to deal equitably with your wives no matter how eager you may be (to do so) ...
>
> *Qur'an 4:129 (The Qur'an. Basic Teachings, p.201)*

DOES ISLAM ALLOW DIVORCE?

Divorce is disliked, but is permitted, and is relatively easy (at least for men) under Islamic law. Muhammad said that divorce was the most hateful of permitted things and Muslim couples should try to be reconciled before making any final decisions about splitting up. The families usually do their best to keep the marriage going, since they were the ones who had arranged it in the first place. If the couple cannot work things out, they should get two arbitrators to help, one to represent each party.

If the couple do decide to get a divorce they must wait three months to see whether or not the woman is pregnant, since the husband must provide for the children of the marriage. On divorce, the marriage dowry must be paid up in full, unless it was the woman who wanted the divorce and was at fault. Generally, Muslim women can ask for divorce only if they have had this right written into their marriage contract.

Divorce is regarded as very serious because marriage and the family provide the framework for Islamic life. Islam only allows it because it accepts human nature and recognises that a marriage relationship may not work. It is considered preferable to divorce and remarry than to be forced to continue with an unhappy marriage and perhaps be tempted to commit adultery. Adultery is seen as a far worse threat to society; Saudi Arabia and Iran impose the death penalty for it on married people, in accordance with Shari'ah.

Is it different for Muslims living in non-Muslim countries?

Wherever Muslims live, they must obey the laws of that country on marriage and divorce. Many Muslims live in countries where family law is based on the Shari'ah; but others find themselves subject to non-Islamic laws, especially those Muslims living in the West.

In Britain, for example, polygamy is illegal. So, if a Muslim already has a wife, he cannot marry any more wives in Britain. If, however, he has legally married more than one wife abroad, there is nothing to stop him living with all his wives in Britain, but only his first wife will be entitled in any legal benefits.

Divorce is subject to British law, although Muslim immigrants could return to their homeland for a divorce, which would then be recognised in Britain.

The lowest age of consent for sex and marriage in Britain is 16, but it is often lower than this in Muslim countries. Muslims are not allowed to live in Britain with younger brides whom they have married abroad.

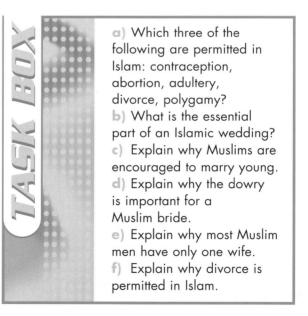

TASK BOX

a) Which three of the following are permitted in Islam: contraception, abortion, adultery, divorce, polygamy?
b) What is the essential part of an Islamic wedding?
c) Explain why Muslims are encouraged to marry young.
d) Explain why the dowry is important for a Muslim bride.
e) Explain why most Muslim men have only one wife.
f) Explain why divorce is permitted in Islam.

HOW DOES ISLAM REGARD THE ELDERLY?

It is customary for a Muslim wife to live with her husband's family – and for their sons to bring home their wives. In an extended family like this, everyone contributes to family life and everyone is provided for. As people grow old, they need to be cared for, and there are many passages in the Qur'an and Hadith encouraging people to look after their parents in their old age.

> Your Lord has enjoined you to worship none but Him, and to show kindness to your parents. If either or both of them attain old age in your dwelling, show them no sign of impatience, nor rebuke them; but speak to them kind words. Treat them with humility and tenderness and say:
> 'Lord, be merciful to them. They nursed me when I was an infant.'
>
> *Qur'an 17:23–4 (The Koran, Penguin Classics, 1974, p.235)*

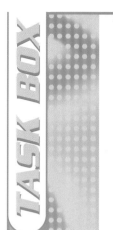

TASK BOX

Discuss the following:

a) What would you say is the attitude of your society to the elderly? Give examples.

b) How would you justify the view that the elderly should be cherished and valued?

PERSPECTIVES

Nadia (the girl who wrote the book about fasting, which was quoted on p.58), now 13, is asked: 'Can you think of any aspect of Islam or Muslim family life that you would like others to know about?' This is how she replied:

Respect for older people in the family is something that I think is a good idea. I also don't think that by the time you're 16 you're really an adult and able to move away from home. In a Muslim family we keep together and support each other, perhaps much more than some families from other cultures. I don't know what my friends think about older people but certainly in a Muslim family I wouldn't dare to be rude to my parents or grandparents. We talk things over and come to a compromise.

RE Today

WHAT HAPPENS WHEN A MUSLIM DIES?

▲ Dying

When a Muslim is dying, the family gathers round to read the Qur'an and say prayers. The dying person should affirm his or her faith, by saying the familiar words of the Kalimah:

There is no god but Allah,
and Muhammad is the Messenger of Allah.

If the person is unable to say this, it will be recited by someone else there.

▲ The corpse

The dead body is washed at least three times. This is done either by the spouse or by someone of the same gender. The first parts of the body to be washed are those that are washed before prayer. The hair (and beard) is perfumed, and also the parts of the body which touch the floor in prostration: the forehead, nose, palms of the hands, knees and feet. The body is wrapped in a shroud: three pieces of white cloth for a man, five for a woman. Alternatively, the ihram may be used if the dead person had completed the Hajj. The face is left uncovered. All this may be done at the mosque if there is a mortuary there.

▲ The funeral

The burial takes place as soon as possible after death. This is done out of respect for the dead, particularly in hot countries where the body can quickly decay. It also has the effect of concentrating the grief felt by the bereaved into a relatively short period, rather than upsetting them all over again if the burial is delayed. Usually only men attend the funeral, as it is thought that women might become too emotional. The body is taken either to the mosque or to the cemetery for the funeral prayer (called the **Salat al-Janazah**). The men line up behind the imam and pray standing, asking for Allah's forgiveness for the dead person's sins. This is important, if the person is to go to heaven.

▲ A Muslim grave

Cremation is forbidden in Islam because Muslims expect Allah to raise up their bodies from the graves on the Last Day. The body is therefore buried. It is laid in the grave with the head turned to the right side, facing Makkah. In hot, dry countries, a coffin is not necessary. Where a coffin is used, the lid is left off if the law permits this. As the grave is filled in with handfuls of earth, passages from the Qur'an are recited. With the first three handfuls, the following verse of the Qur'an is spoken in Arabic:

> We belong to Allah, and to him we return.
>
> *Qur'an 2:156*

Most Muslims have only a mound of earth and a simple headstone to mark the burial place. Shi'ahs have more elaborate graves.

As the mourners walk from the grave, it is a practice to turn and recite the Kalimah again, to make sure the dead person does not forget his or her religion. It is believed that two angels will come to take charge of the dead person's soul until the Day of Resurrection. They will ask three questions:

'Who is your God?'

'Who is your Prophet?'

'What is your religion?'

Muslims should not make too much of their grief, since they should trust in Allah's promises of an after-life and show their acceptance of his will. The period of mourning is no more than three days. Muslims seek strength from the Qur'an during their bereavement, and pray for the dead person. A common prayer is this:

> Peace be upon you; may Allah forgive us all. You went to him before us and we will follow you.
>
> *Milestones, p.120*

▲ Muslims turn to the Qur'an during bereavement.

Another common saying, when thinking of the dead, is from the Qur'an:

> Out of the earth We created you, and We shall restore you into it and bring you forth from it a second time.
>
> *Qur'an 20:57 (Arberry)*

This shows that Muslims are taught to trust in Allah's goodness, and to accept death as a stage in their life and not the end of it.

Muslims believe that the length of a person's life on earth is in God's hands. It is therefore wrong for anyone to shorten human life, except through the due process of law. Therefore both murder and suicide are considered wrong. Euthanasia, sometimes called mercy killing, is also considered to be wrong. The Qur'an states:

> No one dies unless Allah permits. The term of every life is fixed.
>
> *Qur'an 3:145 (The Koran, Penguin Classics, 1974, p.420)*

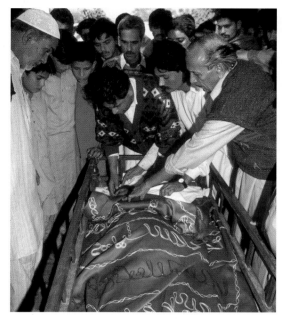

▲ Family and friends pay their respects as the dead body is prepared for burial.

TEST YOURSELF

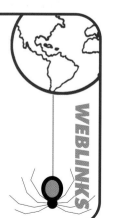

1. Why is the Khalimah important to the dying Muslim?
2. What is unusual about the Salah al-Janazah, compared to the performance of salah at other times?
3. How might you recognise a Muslim area in a cemetery in Britain?
4. Why are bereaved Muslims not supposed to grieve too much?

REMEMBER

▶ Islam guides the whole of a Muslim's life, from birth to death.
▶ Ceremonies are performed for birth, marriage and death.
▶ Marriage is very important for Muslims as the rightful place for sex and bringing up children.
▶ Muslims respect and care for the elderly within the extended family.

1 a) What does Islam teach about the sanctity of life, and how does this affect Islamic laws on abortion, suicide and euthanasia?

b) Explain why the Shari'ah is important for Muslims.

c) 'The world would be a better place if everyone followed God's laws.' What do you think? Give reasons for your opinion, showing that you have considered different points of view.

Assignment

🕸 www.islamia.com
(for information on family marriage and parenting)
🕸 www.ummah.net/social

WEBLINKS

Maulid ul Nabi   Unit 3
The Prophet's Birthday

Laylat-ul-Qadr   Unit 3
The Night of Power, commemorating the first revelation of the Qur'an

Isra'wal Miraj   Unit 3
Commemorating the Night Journey and Ascension of the Prophet

1 Muharram   Unit 3
New Year's Day, celebrating the Hijrah

Id-ul-Fitr   Unit 5
The Festival at the end of Ramadan

Id-ul-Adha   Unit 6
The Festival at the end of Hajj

Months (29/30 days)	Commemorations
1 Muharram	1st The Day of Hijrah; New Year
2 Safar	
3 Rabi ul Awwal	12th Maulid ul Nabi (Birthday of the Prophet)
4 Rabi ul Akhir	
5 Jamada al Awwal	
6 Jamada al Akhir	
7 Rajab	27th Isra' wal Mi'raj (Night Journey and Ascension)
8 Sha'ban	
9 Ramadan	27th Laylat-ul-Qadr (Night of Power)
10 Shawwal	1st Id-ul-Fitr (Minor Festival)
11 Dhul Qi'da	
12 Dhul-Hijjah	10th Id-ul-Adha (Major Festival)

▲ The Islamic calendar.

USEFUL ADDRESSES AND WEBSITES

The Muslim Council of Britain
www.mcb.org.uk/member.html
Membership list of The Muslim Council of Britain, listing many useful Islamic organisations.

Muslim Directory, 65a Grosvenor Road, London W7 1HR
Guide to services and businesses for the Muslim Community, including mosques.

IQRA Trust, 3rd floor, 16 Grosvenor Crescent, London SW1X 7EP 020 7838 7987
www.iqratrust.org
A leading British Muslim educational charity engaged in education and information on Islam. It works with LEAs and schools in many ways to provide accurate information about Islam. It has an enquiry service, a wide range of publications and an Interactive Islamic Experience Exhibition.

The Islamic Cultural Centre and London Central Mosque, 146 Park Road, London NW8 7RG
www.iccuk.org
Websites include a history of this mosque, its prayer-times, etc.

The Islamic Foundation, Markfield Conference Centre, Ratby Lane, Markfield, Leicester LE6 0RN 01530 244944
www.islamic-foundation.com
UK-based institution for education, research, publications and training on Islam; works with inter-faith groups.

Islamic Relief, 151b Park Road, London NW8 7WW
www.islamic-relief.org.uk
International relief and development agency working to alleviate poverty and suffering among some of the world's poorest people, particularly Muslim communities.

Muslim Aid
www.muslimaid.org
International relief and development agency working to alleviate poverty and suffering among some of the world's poorest people.

Arabic Word List

'Abd lit. 'servant' – often used as the first part of a name, for example, Abdullah

adhan first call to prayer

akhirah life after death

al-Amin 'the Trustworthy' – a name given to Muhammad when he was a young man

al-hamdu-li-Llah 'All praise be to Allah'

Allah 'The God' – the Muslim name for God

Allah Subhana wa Ta'ala 'Allah, Glorified and Exalted'

Allahu Akbar 'Allah is the Greatest' – the devotional phrase most frequently on Muslim lips

aqiqah birth ceremonies

Asr the late afternoon prayer

As-Salamu-Alaykum 'Peace be with you' – a common Muslim greeting

ayah a unit within a surah of the Qur'an

Ayatollah lit. 'Sign of Allah' – title of a leader of the Twelver Shi'is

Bismillah (variant: **Basmalah**) 'In the name of Allah' – the beginning of a phrase which starts all the chapters of the Qur'an except the ninth

caliph 'successor' to Muhammad

Dar-ul-Islam lit. 'House of Islam' – the Muslim empire

Dar-ul-Uloom 'House of Knowledge' – an Islamic college

Dawud David

dhikr 'remembrance' – repetition of the name of Allah

Dhul-Hijjah twelfth month of the Islamic calendar, the pilgrimage month

du'a lit. 'asking' – a personal prayer

Fajr the dawn prayer

fard obligatory

Fatihah lit. 'Opening' – title of the first chapter of the Qur'an

Hadith lit. 'statement' – collection of authenticated reports of what Muhammad said, did or approved

hafiz a man who has learnt the whole Qur'an by heart

hafizah a woman who has learnt the whole Qur'an by heart

Hajj lit. 'to set out for a definite purpose' – name of the Greater Pilgrimage to Makkah, the Fifth Pillar of Islam

hajja a woman who has completed Hajj

hajji a man who has completed Hajj

halal permitted

Hanif lit. 'one who is inclined', i.e. to believe in the One God, a monotheist

haram forbidden/sacred

Hijrah 'Emigration' of the Muslims to Yathrib/Madinah and the beginning of the Islamic calendar

Ibrahim Abraham

id festival

idi a festival gift

Id Mubarak 'Happy Festival' i.e. a festival greeting

Id-ul-Adha 'Great Festival', the Festival of Sacrifice at the end of Hajj

Id-ul-Fitr 'Festival of Fast Breaking' at the end of Ramadan

iftar meal which breaks the fast

ihram lit. 'consecration' – name for the pilgrim's clothes

ijma consensus of Islamic scholars

imam lit. 'in the front' – the prayer leader (who stands in front of the other worshippers)

Imam title for the leader of the Shi'ahs

Injil the (Christian) Gospel

Insha Allah 'If Allah is willing'

'iqamah second call to prayer, just before prayer begins

Isa Jesus

Isha the night prayer

Islam the religion of the Muslims, meaning 'peace' through 'submission' to Allah

Isra' wal Mi'raj the Night Journey and Ascension of Muhammad into heaven

Jebreel Gabriel

jihad lit. 'striving', i.e. against evil, holy war

jinn a spirit said to live in natural places like springs, trees and caves

Jumu'ah lit. 'assembly' or 'congregation'; the Jumu'ah prayer is the Friday midday prayer

Ka'bah lit. 'cube' – the name of the cube-shaped building in the centre of the Sacred Mosque at Makkah, believed to be the first house of worship of the One God.

Kalimah 'statement' of faith – refers to the First Pillar of Islam

Khadijah the name of Muhammad's first wife

khalifah successor, inheritor, custodian

khatib preacher of the Firday sermon

khitan circumcision

khutbah the Friday sermon

kiswah the cloth that covers the Ka'bah

Laylat-ul-Qadr the Night of Power when Muhammad is said to have received his first revelation of the Qur'an

Madinah the 'Town (of the Prophet)' where Muhammad spent his last ten years

madrasah Islamic school or college

Maghrib the sunset prayer

Mahdi the divinely 'guided' one expected to appear before the Day of Judgement

mahr wedding dowry paid by the bridegroom

Makkah (variant: **Mecca**) the holiest city for Muslims

masjid (known in English as **mosque**) lit. 'place of prostration'

Masjid al-Haram the Sacred Mosque in Makkah

Maulid ul Nabi Birthday of the Prophet

mihrab alcove in a wall of a mosque to indicate the direction for prayer

minbar the raised preaching platform in a mosque

minaret tower near or attached to a mosque, from which the call to prayer is sounded

mubarak 'happy', as in the festival greeting 'Id Mubarak'

mu'adhin (known in English as **muezzin**) the person who sounds the prayer call

Muharram first month of the Islamic calendar

Musa Moses

Muslim lit. 'one who surrenders' to Allah – a follower of Islam

nabi prophet

niyyah lit. 'intention' – concentrating the mind in preparation for worshipping Allah

qadar Allah's complete and final control over the fulfilment of events or destiny

qiblah the 'direction' for prayer, facing towards the Ka'bah, in Makkah

qiyam standing (in prayer)

Qur'an lit. 'recitation' – name of the holy book of Islam, believed to have been revealed through Muhammad, who recited it to others

rak'ah a cycle or unit of prayer, both words and actions

Ramadan ninth month of the Islamic calendar, the month of fasting

rasul messenger of Allah, i.e. a prophet who brought a book

riba interest (on savings or loans)

risala prophecy

ruku bowing (in prayer)

sadaqah voluntary charity

sahih lit. 'sound' – referring to Hadith

Sa'y ritual 'Running' between Mounts As-Safa and Al-Marwa, on pilgrimage

sajdah prostrating (in prayer)

salah ritual prayer to be done five times a day, the Second Pillar of Islam

Salat al-Id festival prayer session

Salat al-Janazah the funeral prayer

salam 'peace' – final movement in the rak'ah

sawm 'fasting' in the month of Ramadan, the Fourth Pillar of Islam

Shahadah 'declaration' of faith, the First Pillar of Islam

Shari'ah Islamic law based on the Qur'an and Sunnah

Shi'ahs, Shi'is or Shi'ites a minority of Muslims, who belong to the 'party of Ali'

shirk sin of idolatry; the worst sin for Muslims

subhah prayer beads

Subhan Allah 'Glory be to Allah'

suf wool – perhaps where the Sufis got their name

Sunnah the 'way' or 'custom' of the Prophet, i.e. the example he set for Muslims to follow

Sunni the majority of Muslims, who claim to follow the right 'path' of Islam

surah chapter of the Qur'an

tariqah the Sufi way or path

tawhid the oneness of Allah

Tawaf ritual 'Circling' of the Ka'bah

Tawrah/Tawrat the (Jewish) Torah

'ulama religious lawyers

Ummah the worldwide Muslim community

Umrah the Lesser Pilgrimage to Makkah, which can be done at any time

wudu ritual washing before prayer

Zabur the Book of Psalms

zakah poor-due, the Third Pillar of Islam

Zakat-ul-Fitr the poor-due at Id-ul-Fitr

Zuhr the noon prayer

INDEX